P9-DNP-201

For the Healing
of the Nations

For the Healing of the Nations

The Book of Revelation
in an Age of Cultural Conflict

Justo L. González

ORBIS BOOKS

Maryknoll, New York 10545

The Catholic Foreign Mission Society of America (Maryknoll) recruits and trains people for overseas missionary service. Through Orbis Books, Maryknoll aims to foster the international dialogue that is essential to mission. The books published, however, reflect the opinions of their authors and are not meant to represent the official position of the society. To obtain further information about Maryknoll and Orbis Books, please visit our website at www.maryknoll.org.

Copyright ©1999 by Justo L. González

All rights reserved. No part of this publication may be reproduced or transmitted in any form or by any means, electronic or mechanical, including photocopying, recording or any information storage or retrieval system, without prior permission in writing from Orbis Books, P. O. Box 308, Maryknoll, New York 10545-0308, U.S.A.

Manufactured in the United States of America

Library of Congress Cataloging-in-Publication Data

González, Justo L.
    For the healing of the nations : the book of Revelation in an age of cultural conflict / Justo L. González.
        p.   cm.
    Includes bibliographical references and index.
    ISBN 1-57075-273-7 (pbk.)
    1. Bible. N.T. Revelation—Criticism, interpretation, etc.
2. Hope—Religious aspects—Christianity—History of doctrines—
Early church, ca. 30–600. 3. Culture conflict—Religious aspects—
Christianity—History of doctrines—Early church, ca. 30–600.
    I. Title
BS2825.2.C84G66   1999
228'.06—dc21   99-32198
                                                                      CIP

Contents

Preface

The book of Revelation has held a strange fascination over Christians for centuries. Ancient illuminated manuscripts, medieval cathedrals, and even modern-day movies are full of images drawn from this strange book. From it, hard pressed Christians through the ages have drawn strength and comfort. From it, interpreters of great—but very prosaic—imagination have drawn schemes and charts about the impending end of the world. Today, however, the vast majority of "mainline" Christians in the supposedly "more advanced" parts of the world shy away from it, apparently for fear of wild lucubrations such as led to the events in Jonestown, Guyana, or Waco, Texas.

I am convinced, however, that this avoidance of the book of Revelation is also based on a deeper, unconfessed fear that the sort of Christianity depicted there may be too exacting for us; that it may make demands on us and on our churches to which we are not ready to respond.

That fear is well founded. Revelation makes very clear that there are hard choices to be made, and that in these choices quite often there is no middle ground.

On the other hand, Revelation is essentially a book of hope. It is a book of promise. It rings with notes that have inspired many a hymn. It is a poem to God's future, and to our future with God. It offers a hope so great that it can be described only in terms of poetry and metaphor. It promises liberation from the injustices that the oppressed suffer, from the fears that haunt the oppressors, from the anguish of those in between, and from the pain and misery of all.

The net result of all of this is that many Christians deprive themselves of the hope the book offers for fear of what it may demand.

Then there are those who simply classify the book as "apocalyptic" and immediately relegate it to that corner of history reserved for the curious, but irrelevant. We are then told that the book reflects strange notions that circulated in the first century, but that have nothing to do with us. Following that line of thought, even though we do not quite rip Revelation out of our Bibles, for all practical intents that is what we in fact do.

On the other hand, the more I read and study the book of Revelation, the more convinced I become of its relevance for today—indeed, the more relevant I find it for my own life and that of my own community.

It is out of these experiences that the present book was formed. In its earlier form, the core of the argument was presented in lectures at Brite Divinity School, Wesley Theological Seminary, Iliff School of Theology, Austin Presbyterian Theological Seminary, and Nanjing Theological Seminary. Part of it—especially the sections on eschatology—was originally presented jointly by my wife, Catherine, and me in a series of lectures at Southern Baptist Seminary on preaching about Revelation—given under the title of "The Butler Did It: Preaching the Mystery When You Know the End." At each of these various presentations, colleagues and students have asked questions or made suggestions that have further enriched my own thoughts on this fascinating book of the Bible. I now publish this material with the hope and the prayer that it too may become part of a larger conversation for the good of the church and the healing of the nations.

Justo L. González
Decatur, Georgia
October 1998

I

Garlic Wars?
Culture and Conflict
in the Twenty-first Century

"It smells of garlic!" my companion commented as he frowned in disgust.

"Yes, it does!" I responded, smiling as I took in the delicious aroma.

There it was all in a nutshell—the cultural conflicts that threaten to tear the world apart as we drift into the twenty-first century. We were walking into a church, the church where his mother had been baptized and his grandparents had been married. The congregation is mostly white, very active in evangelism and fairly progressive on social issues. Decades earlier they had participated actively in the civil rights movement, and now they had decided to open the church to their new immigrant neighbors from the Caribbean. It was not an easy decision, for there were many in the community who blamed the new immigrants for declining property values and overcrowding in the schools. But they had made the decision that they felt they should make

1

as committed Christians, and now there was a flourishing
Spanish-speaking congregation sharing the facilities with
the older English-speaking one. In the discussion leading to
this decision, prophets of doom had spoken of many reasons
why the arrangement would not work. They had worried
about race, language, age differences, education, and much
more. But no one had even thought of garlic!

And yet, as my friend and I walked into the building,
garlic became a symbol of the world in which we shall have
to live in the twenty-first century. How can garlic lovers and
garlic haters share the same space?

This example illustrates several points that are important to remember as we deal with issues of culture and the
encounter of cultures in the twenty-first century.

First of all, it reminds us that, in spite of all attempts,
culture is undefinable. Anthropologists have offered all sorts
of definitions of culture; but in the final analysis culture, as
any human phenomenon, is undefinable. Certainly, a culture is the manner in which a given people responds to the
challenges of the world: challenges of survival (food production, diet, shelter, clothing), challenges of communication
(language and social relations), and challenges of meaning
(art, myth, values, religion). Yet these intersect in such a
multitude of ways that every theoretical definition must
yield to factual reality. We cannot fully and strictly define
culture. We cannot tell exactly where one culture begins
and another ends. And yet, culture is there. As the ancient
philosopher would say, "movement is proven by walking."

Second, culture is much more than its "cultured" elements—its poetry, art, etc. Culture is also garlic, rice, and
olive oil, or meat, lard, and potatoes. Culture is what the
most "uncultured" peasant does when constructing a shelter

for his family, what his wife does when threading a loom, and the manner in which both react to the birth of a child. Third, the learning of a culture is not only a matter of will. My friend may be convinced that he must come to like the smell of garlic. He may try to get used to it. And still, he may or may not succeed. I write in English as often and as easily as I do in my native Spanish, and therefore to a certain extent I am bilingual and bicultural. And yet, English poetry does not stir me as it does others. I try to like it. People tell me it is beautiful. Sometimes I am moved by it—but never as much as by poetry in Spanish. (Once I found a poem by Longfellow I truly enjoyed, and then discovered that he had translated it from Spanish!)

Finally, and most important for our purposes here, since cultures imply an entire world view, they seek to occupy the same space, like the garlic lovers and the garlic haters in that church. For a culture simply to ignore another does not make it easier to coexist. The garlic haters may be very tolerant, but every time they walk into the church they will be confronted with the smell of garlic. On the other hand, if the garlic lovers ignore the garlic haters, the latter will in the end hate them! Accommodation may be possible—the garlic lovers may cook elsewhere, may run an exhaust fan, etc., and the garlic haters may wear more perfume. But coexistence is not possible without adjustment.

It is for this reason that the subject of the encounter of cultures, and the conflict among cultures, will be so important in the century that is now dawning. In times past, the encounter of cultures was not as constant nor as complex as it is today. Until fairly recently, the speed of human travel was limited to the speed of the horse—and it had remained fairly constant for millennia. Apart from carrier pigeons, telegraph signal towers, drums, and smoke signals, ideas could not travel without human conveyance. Today, this has changed drastically. I can be halfway around the world in a few hours. I can pick up the phone and dial someone in Nairobi just as easily as I can dial my next-door neighbor. Electronic mail and the Internet allow me to visit the Vatican Library or to purchase a book in Taiwan. When my neighbors, who do not know a word of Spanish, flip through their television channels, they cannot avoid hearing Spanish—and in some cases Japanese and Korean. Thus, political borders have become more permeable to cross-cultural influxes, even apart from the actual migration of peoples.

That migration, however, cannot be ignored. For many reasons—political and military upheavals, economic inequities, intellectual quests, natural disaster, and sheer wanderlust—during the last decades people have been moving across political and cultural borders at an unprecedented rate. When I first moved to Atlanta in 1969, it was difficult to find other Spanish-speaking people. Today, Spanish is heard regularly in stores, theaters, and streets. The buying power of Latinos in the United States, which most companies ignored a decade ago, has now surpassed $350 billion. By the year 2010, it is expected that 15.5 percent of the entire population of the United States (not even counting Puerto Rico) will be Hispanic. Other minorities in the United States, notably the Koreans, are increasing at an even faster rate.

Although the news media often give the impression that this is exclusively an American phenomenon, as if everybody in the world were moving to the United States, the unprecedented migration of people is a worldwide phenomenon. Indeed, it began at the dawn of the modern age, with the migration of Europeans, first to the Western Hemisphere, and then to South Africa, Australia, New Zealand, and the rest of the world. By the middle of the twentieth century, there were significant European and North-American enclaves in practically every region of the world. Then, in the second half of that century, the current began to reverse, with people moving from the South (Asia, Africa, Latin America) to the North (Europe, the United States, Canada) as well as to the traditional Northern enclaves in the South (Australia, New Zealand). As one travels through Europe, it is not unusual to hear Arabic and Swahili in the streets of Paris, Turkish in Berlin, and Malay or Batak in Amsterdam. Chinese is spoken in Jakarta, Lima, and the interior of Bolivia.

Without the growing ease in communications that was taking place at the same time, many of these immigrants would have been rapidly assimilated into the dominant culture of the area where they settled, much as the earlier Italian immigrants to the United States became assimilated, losing their language and many of their traditional customs. But constant communication with the country of origin and the possibility of periodic visits back and forth have made it possible for the new immigrants to retain much of their traditional culture and even to pass it on to their children.

Furthermore, since many immigrants tend to be younger than the average native of the land into which they move, their birthrate tends to be higher, thus producing a further increase in the immigrant population. In 1994, for instance, the U.S. Census Bureau reported that the median age of Latinos in the United States was twenty-four years, compared with thirty-five for the rest of the population. While the majority of the population was beyond its peak reproductive years, the majority of the Hispanic population was precisely at that peak. Consequently, even if immigration were to halt completely, the Latino population would continue to grow at a faster rate than the rest of the population. (This does not even take into account the fact that, both for cultural and for economic reasons, the birthrate among Latinos is higher than that among people of the same age in the dominant culture.)

Clearly, cultures do not exist in isolation from each other. If a culture is the way in which a particular people respond to the challenges of their world and their environment, then other cultures must be seen as part of that environment. Jewish post-Hellenistic culture was not the same as the Jewish culture of Ezra. The Egyptian culture of the first century, under Roman rule, was not the same as the Egyptian culture of the Twelfth Dynasty. Likewise, the cultures that have emerged at the end of the colonial age bear the mark of the colonial period, and therefore are better equipped to cope with the challenges of the still dominant cultures of the North Atlantic. It is precisely this resilience that makes these emerging cultures appear as a serious threat to the dominant cultures of the North, which—precisely as a result of their dominance—have not had to develop the same level of adaptability. (Returning to the case of the garlic lovers and garlic haters, the garlic lovers, precisely because they are immigrants and have a long history of adapting and coping, are probably better equipped to deal with the issues at hand than garlic haters such as my friend, whose grandparents were married in that church.)

In short, then, what the entire world is facing as we enter the third millennium is the prospect of a multiplicity of cultures attempting to share the same space, much as the garlic lovers and the garlic haters must share the same church building. A few decades ago, people could sing with romantic nostalgia about "faraway places with strange sounding names." Today we do not have to look to faraway places with exotic names such as Islamabad, Tananarive, or Quetzaltenango to find diversity; we can find that diversity and sometimes even a clash of cultures and traditions in places with names such as Orange County, New York City, or Fort Worth, Texas. Moreover, the reemergence of previously submerged cultures is not taking place only in the traditional homelands of those cultures, for we are speaking not only of a renascent Arabic culture in Arabia or Libya, but of one that confronts us in our own backyards; not of the rebirth of Mayan myths and practices in Copán, but of their presence in Texas and Chicago; not of Afro-Caribbean rites and traditions in Haiti, but of animal sacrifices in Florida.

Culture, however, does not exist in isolation of economics and politics. The cultural migrations of our day are deeply connected to economic oppression and political upheaval. When seen from different cultural and social perspectives, the decades leading to the third millennium may appear as both the best of times and the worst of times.

In general, from the perspective of North-Atlantic culture, the last decades of the nineteenth century and most of the twentieth century were a golden age—much as the first and second centuries of the Christian era were a golden age for the Roman Empire. The golden age of our own era was the time of many of the advances in speed of travel and communication that were mentioned above. It was also a time of unprecedented advances in industrial production and military technology—if the latter can really be called "advances." Most of these were in the hands of the North-

Atlantic powers, and therefore this was also a period of unprecedented political and economic expansion for what
came to be known as "the West." Kenneth Scott Latourette
has bluntly summarized these events:

> Now, in the nineteenth century, Europeans ex-
> plored and subjugated Africa, they completed the
> conquest of India and Ceylon, they blasted open the
> doors of China and threatened to partition that em-
> pire among themselves, they induced the Japanese
> to admit their merchants, diplomats, and missionar-
> ies, they made themselves masters of the islands of
> the Pacific, and in Australia and New Zealand built
> new nations of European stock, they further devel-
> oped Siberia, and they completed their occupation
> of the Americas. By A.D. 1914 all the land surface
> of the world was politically subject to European
> peoples except a few spots in Africa, some of the
> Asiatic states, Japan, a little corner of South-eastern
> Europe, and the jungles in the interior of some of
> the largest of the islands of the Pacific. Even the
> lands which had not submitted politically had been
> touched by the commerce of Europeans and most
> of them had been modified by European culture.[1]

What had begun in the nineteenth century continued
into the latter half of the twentieth, sometimes as further
political expansion, but most often in the form of neocolo-

---

[1]*The Great Century in Europe and the United States of America*, vol.
4 of *A History of the Expansion of Christianity* (New York: Harper &
Brothers, 1941), 13.

nialism. The industrialized nations had learned that overt colonial rule was not necessary in order to reap the benefits of colonialism. As a result, while the second half of the twentieth century saw a sharp decline in colonial rule, it also witnessed the increased globalization of the economic order, to the point that only the remotest regions of the globe were not impacted by that globalization—which in turn benefited the former centers of colonial rule. Thus, while colonialism waned, neocolonialism continued expanding to the very end of the twentieth century.

This enormous expansion, like the earlier expansion of the Roman Empire, did not take place without the acquiescence and even collaboration of many in the conquered and occupied territories. Indeed, many of the traditional elites of such territories increased their power and wealth through this process, which also resulted in the creation of new native elites. The case of India may serve as an example for what took place throughout the world. That the colonial powers had a stake in the preservation of the traditional elites was acknowledged as a matter of policy by the first British viceroy after the Sepoy Mutiny, Lord Canning: "If we could keep up a number of Native States without political power, but as royal instruments, we should exist in India as long as our naval supremacy was maintained." Almost eighty years later, the Maharajah of Mymensingh confirmed the symbiotic relationship between his interests and those of the colonial power: "If we are to exist as a class, it is our duty to strengthen the hold of the [British] Government."[2] Also in India, as elsewhere, the colonial power developed a

---

[2]Both quoted in L. S. Stavrianos, *Global Rift: The Third World Comes of Age* (New York: William Morrow and Co., 1981), 238.

new elite, mostly through its vast system of schools, which produced "a new class of Indians familiar with foreign languages and cultures, and committed to liberal and rational ideologies."[3] As we shall see, there are parallels between these policies and results and the policies and results of first-century Roman imperialism.

On the other hand, as was also the case with Roman imperialism, the *pax Britannica* and the *pax Americana* were only such from a certain perspective. Still using India as an example, it is significant that it was Viceroy Lord Minto who purposefully introduced into Indian politics the custom of separate voting systems for Hindus and Muslims, thus forcing the two groups to work constantly at odds with each other, and eventually leading to the partition of the subcontinent. Repeatedly, in various parts of the world, the colonial powers armed rival clans and tribes against each other, much as in an earlier time the Native Americans had been armed in order to fight as proxies for the British, the Colonials, or the French. Eventually, mostly during the second half of the twentieth century, most of the former colonies would gain their political independence, many of them through bloody struggles that would be followed by civil strife, dictatorship, and further bloodshed. During most of the second half of the twentieth century, the North divided itself between what it called "East" and "West," thus providing the ideology for a "Cold War" which was often quite hot in the so-called "Third World." Significantly, even after the collapse of the "East," or "Second World," the poorer nations, or "Third World," continued being third, even though there was no longer a second! Thus, the title of Stavrianos's

---

[3]Ibid., 239.

study of these developments accurately describes the condition of the world at the beginning of the third millennium: *Global Rift: The Third World Comes of Age.* In the course of this process, there came a time when it seemed that the ancient cultures were doomed. They could not resist the impact of Western culture and civilization. Writing at the end of World War II, Kenneth Scott Latourette declared:

> Out of the world-wide expansion of Europe and the transformation of non-European cultures through contact with the West came...the beginning of a world culture. This world culture was an extension of the civilization of Europe.[4]

Once again, this reminds us of the cosmopolitan culture that resulted first from the conquests of Alexander and then from Roman expansion. Underlying that cosmopolitan culture, however, were the ancient cultures of the conquered peoples, ready to emerge at an opportune moment. Likewise, underlying the supposedly cosmopolitan culture of the twentieth century were the various cultures of the colonized peoples, ready to emerge once again.

At any rate, just as in the ancient world there was, as we shall see in the next chapter, a "period of manifest Greek dominance and oriental submersion," and then a "period of reaction of a renascent East," so also in our more recent history there was a period of manifest Western dominance over the cultures of the colonized South, followed by a current period of reaction of a renascent South.

---

[4]*The Great Century in Europe*, 14.

The breakdown of colonialism brought about the creation of dozens of new states. The independent nations of the world, some four dozen at the beginning of the twentieth century, now number approximately two hundred, and that number is still growing. This was not accomplished without pain and violence. That is the main thrust of Daniel Patrick Moynihan's book, appropriately entitled *Pandemonium: Ethnicity in International Politics*. After commenting on the role of ethnicity and cultural diversity in the breakdown of the Soviet Union, Moynihan continues:

> Yugoslavia came apart also, beginning with a brutal clash between Serbia and Croatia, here again "nations" with only the smallest differences in genealogy; with, indeed, practically a common language. Ethnic conflict does not require great differences; small will do. In late 1991, two rival Nigerian groups, the Tiv and Jukun, both primarily Christian, took to fighting over farmland. The resulting deaths in the thousands were barely reported in the West. Deaths in the tens of thousands followed the escalation of civil war in 1991 between clans in Somalia, a country of some six million persons speaking the same language, most of them Sunni Muslims. Hawike, Darod, Isaaks slaughtered one another as children starved.[5]

Furthermore, cultural and ethnic conflict has become a factor, not only in the creation of new nations, but also in the everyday life of cities in the North-Atlantic West. After riots in Los Angeles in which African-Americans vented their

---

[5]Daniel Patrick Moynihan, *Pandemonium: Ethnicity in International Politics* (Oxford University Press, 1993), 15-16.

anger on Koreans, a conservative journalist commented: "The United States is unwinding strand by strand, rather like the Soviet Union, Yugoslavia, or Northern Ireland."[6] Needless to say, the implication of all this is that human tribalism is such that, left to our own devices, we shall devour each other. Therefore, a strong authority is needed to keep the various tribes in check—a strong authority such as the former centralized government in the Soviet Union or the traditional white ruling elite in the United States. The collapse of former unities, no matter how oppressive they may have been, is now seen by many as having opened the floodgates of chaos. The result is a growing nostalgia for universality, which is often confused with catholicity. To the difference between catholicity and universality we shall return shortly. But first, we must look into the reasons for the collapse of the former unities.

What makes such collapses possible? In the first century, it was in part the breakdown of Hellenistic hegemony through Roman expansion. Today, it is in part the breakdown of modernity. Just as the Hellenization of the world was the ideological justification by which Alexander's successors claimed their power, modernity was the ideological justification by which the West (that is, the Northwest) conquered, subjugated, and exploited the rest of the world. Macedonian expansion was built on the metanarrative of Hellenization; Western expansion was built on the metanarrative of modernity.

That metanarrative, like an ellipse, revolved around two foci that constituted its axis: objectivity and universality. True knowledge must be objective, and therefore capable of

---

[6]William Rees-Mogg, "The Sheriff Fiddles While the Town Burns," *Independent*, 5/4/92, 17.

universal recognition. Subjectivity and particularity are inferior to objectivity and universality, and are at best stepping stones on the road to truth. If any do not "yet" accept or understand this objective truth, it is simply because they have not reached the point where it is clear to them. Meanwhile, those who know this universal objective truth have as a task, as their "manifest destiny," the "white man's burden" of conveying it to the unenlightened.

The convincing power of modernity lay first of all in its undeniable successes within a narrow but impressive band in the spectrum of human experience. The natural sciences and their technological applications, which approached the ideal of objective universality more than other disciplines and endeavors, were also able to boast greater achievements. That being the case, it seemed logical that the reason why humankind had not made equal progress in issues of politics, economics, or morality was that these areas were not approached with the same universal objectivity as that applied to physics or mathematics. On this point, Descartes set the mood for modernity when he took geometry as the model for his method:

> Those long chains of totally simple and easy reasonings of which the geometers are accustomed to make use in order to arrive at their most difficult demonstrations had given me occasion to imagine that all those things which can fall under the knowledge of men follow from each other in the same fashion, and that, provided only that one abstain from accepting any of them as true that not be, and that one always keep to the order that is necessary in order to deduce the ones from the others, there

can be none so remote that one not finally reach them, nor so hidden that one not discover them.[7]

Second, the convincing power of modernity lay in sheer physical power. The modern nations of the world, thanks to their superior technology, could conquer others, while convincing themselves that they were doing this for the good of all. As Ashis Nandy has stated, colonialism is the armed version of modernity.[8] Thus, while modernity justified colonialism, the latter seemed to confirm the former's universal vocation. Once again, one is reminded of Hellenization as the justification for Macedonian expansion, and of the latter as a convincing argument for the superiority of Greek culture.

For these reasons, the collapse of modernity is paralleled by the resurgence of cultures that modernity seemed to have not only submerged, but even drowned.

Significantly, however, what is often called "postmodernity" is in large measure a continuation of modernity. Jean-François Lyotard begins his famous opus on postmodernity[9] by stating that he is concerned with the state of knowledge in "the most developed societies." In other words, while proclaiming the demise of the metanarratives of modernity, Lyotard clings to the central features of a Eurocentric metanarrative of "development." In this brave new world with no metanarratives, the former centers of modernity will remain

---

[7]*Discourse on Method*, part 2.11, trans. George Heffernan (Notre Dame: University of Notre Dame Press, 1994), 35.

[8]*The Intimate Enemy: Loss and Recovery of Self under Colonialism* (Delhi: Oxford University Press, 1983).

[9]*La condition postmoderne: Rapport sur le savoir* (Paris: Minuit, 1979).

at the center, and the former margins will remain marginal. Modernity may be on the way out; but its heir is already in place. Once again, one marvels at the parallelism with the Roman Empire moving in to fill the vacuum left by the decline of Hellenism.

There are other players in the field besides modernity and postmodernity, just as there were other cultures and peoples in the first century besides Hellenists and Romans. These are the other cultures, peoples, and traditions that were ignored or suppressed by modernity, and which are now coming forth with new vigor. Claiming to be neither modern nor postmodern, but extramodern, those peoples and cultures that were excluded from the benefits of modernity will not surrender their own metanarratives in order to join the bandwagon of postmodernity.[10]

Significantly, many persons representing the reemerging cultures are also Christian. Most of them became Christian as a result of the impact of modernity and colonialism on their lands—modernity and colonialism which in their religious transmutation took the form of Christian missions. They too have been going through a similar process of moving from modernity to postmodernity—or rather, of claiming their own cultural extramodernity. It is important to note that modernity was being born precisely at the time of the great geographic expansion of Christianity to the Western Hemisphere, and that next wave of expansion, in the nineteenth century and the early twentieth, came at the

---

[10]Along these lines, see my essay, "Metamodern Aliens in Postmodern Jerusalem," in *Hispanic/Latino Theology: Challenge and Promise*, ed. Ada María Isasi-Díaz and Fernando F. Segovia (Minneapolis: Fortress, 1996), 340-50.

time of modernity's greatest successes. Therefore it is not surprising that, just as modernity tended to eclipse the ancestral cultures of other lands, so too modern missions— both Catholic and Protestant—tended to create churches that were carbon copies of their mother churches, with little cognizance of the cultures in which they were implanted.

It must be noted that the Council of Trent, with its emphasis on uniformity and universality, also took place at the very beginning of the Modern Age. Indeed, much of the resistance to the decrees of Trent, notably in France, but also in some quarters in the Spanish colonies and elsewhere, had to do with the universalizing thrust of its decrees. Not only in matters of dogma, but also in matters of organization, worship, and theological curriculum, the church was to be universal—which was understood as being as much as possible the same everywhere. A list of forbidden books was drawn up. Courses of study in theology were prescribed. The Vulgate was declared to be the one official translation of Scripture. As a fitting symbol of this mood, the post-tridentine church enforced Latin as the official language of worship, not only in Western Europe, where it had once been spoken but was now increasingly forgotten, but also in the churches founded more recently in places where Latin had never been spoken, from Mexico to Japan. This universalizing emphasis was further reinforced as the church perceived each modern development as a threat to its teaching or its interests, and culminated in the pontificate of Pius IX, with the *Syllabus of Errors* and the First Vatican Council.

Thus, the relationship of Roman Catholicism to modernity presented a curious paradox. On the one hand, ecclesiastical authorities saw modernity as a constant threat, particularly in its emphasis on free enquiry, democracy, the

secular state, state-sponsored education, etc. This reaction
against modernity grew more acute as the perceived threats
became more pressing, and thus it is fair to say that

> . . . the nineteenth century was—even more than the
> sixteenth—the most conservative century in the his-
> tory of Roman Catholicism. In the face of a rapidly
> changing world the Catholic Church chose—at least
> officially—to formulate an understanding of itself
> that reflected conditions no longer existing in the
> world. In a time of growing skepticism and ques-
> tioning of every authority, the pope was declared in-
> fallible. When the Virgin birth of Jesus was being
> doubted, the pope proclaimed the immaculate con-
> ception of Mary. Europe was being flooded with
> new and radical ideas, and the church still relied on
> the *Index* and the Holy Office to combat those
> ideas. When modern forms of critical research were
> developed, Rome condemned those who tried to re-
> late them to religious questions.[11]

On the other hand, their very understanding of the
unity of the church and their emphasis on uniformity and
universality were typically modern.

The reaction of most branches of Protestantism to
modernity was much more positive, especially among theologians in the nineteenth century. Critical and historical
methods for the study of Scripture were encouraged and almost canonized. Scholars questioned the authorship, dating,

---

[11]Justo L. González, *A History of Christian Thought*, rev. ed. (Nashville: Abingdon, 1987), 3: 410.

and literary integrity, as well as the historical value, of every book in the Bible. There was hardly an item of doctrine that some theologian did not subject to the most demanding critical analysis, either reinterpreting or altogether rejecting it. Theologians sought to prove that Christianity—and more specifically Protestant Christianity—was the modern religion par excellence, and was therefore the natural ally of scientific research, democracy, free enterprise, and other such modern icons.

Meanwhile, there were many in the rank and file of Protestantism who did not accept these modern interpretations of the faith. This resulted in a growing chasm between theologians and the faithful, between scholars and believers, which eventually led to conservative reactions such as fundamentalism and various new orthodoxies. Significantly, however, even these reactions to "modernism" carried within themselves the stamp of modernity, inasmuch as they insisted on the objective, universal character of the faith and of Christian doctrine.

Thus, while the tension within Roman Catholicism was an inner paradox, the tension within Protestantism resulted in divisions that persist to this day.

In both cases, however, the decline of modernity is opening new perspectives, challenges, and opportunities. Although at first many of the newly founded churches of the Modern Age were mere imitations of Western Christianity, what eventually emerged was a multiplicity of cultural incarnations of Christianity, each with its own flavor. As a result, the encounter of cultures in our midst is often also an encounter of various ways of being Christian. The cultural conflicts of our time are also conflicts within the church. The garlic lovers and garlic haters in my friend's church may be culturally alien to each other, but they are both Christian. The challenge of multiculturalism is not only "out there," in society at large, but also within the church.

How we deal with that challenge is crucial to the church and its mission, for at least two reasons. First and foremost, if the Christian community is to be a city set on a hill, or a beacon guiding the world into God's future, its own inner life must point the way toward that future. If the Christian gospel is not powerful enough within the church itself to lead us through the difficulties of ethnic conflict and cultural dissonance, we can hardly claim that it is good news to a world going through similar difficulties on a much larger scale. The church must be one, not primarily for its own sake—or its own order, its own sense of security, etc. The church must be one because a fragmented church is not much help to a fragmented world.

Further, and perhaps only at a very secondary level, the church must deal with its own cultural diversity for the sake of its own well being. In my friend's church, garlic lovers and garlic haters must find a way to be the church together, or not be the church at all.

This is not easy. It is not easy for my friend who dislikes the smell of garlic to tolerate that smell in the church where his mother was baptized—a church in which he grew up amid the smell of roses and gardenias.

And yet, our generation is by no means the first to have to deal with these issues. Indeed, the very first Christian generation had to deal with them. And the people of that generation did not find it easy! They had to struggle over these issues—to struggle so hard and so constantly that this became one of the dominant themes of what we now call the New Testament.

It was in this context that the early church developed its emphasis on catholicity. In spite of what we may have been told, "catholic" is not the same as "universal"; rather, in some contexts, it is its exact opposite![12] Etymologically, "catholic" means "according to the whole," or "according to all." Had Alexander the Great managed to conquer the whole world, his rule would have been universal, but never catholic. Thus, when the early church developed a canon of the New Testament, that canon was "catholic" because it included gospels and other writings that reflected a variety of perspectives and experiences within the church. Starkly stated, although the Gospel of Matthew is fully orthodox and canonical, it by itself would not be the "catholic" witness to the Gospel of Jesus Christ.

True catholicity implies that, as new perspectives are brought into conversation on the Christian faith, new insights into that faith are discovered—much as when different people look at a single landscape, and share with each other what they see, the landscape is enriched for all.

What is true of the Christian faith as a whole is also true of its foundational texts. Indeed, the underlying premise of this entire book is that, out of our constant struggle with issues of culture and ethnicity, we may be able to discern meanings in the New Testament that we would otherwise miss—more specifically, that by looking at the cultural issues underlying the book of Revelation, we may come to see its deep significance for our age.

---

[12]This is a subject I have developed more fully in *Out of Every Tribe and Nation: Christian Theology at the Ethnic Roundtable* (Nashville: Abingdon, 1992), 18-37.

II

Culture and Conflict
in the First Century

Edward Gibbon begins his famous *History of the Decline and Fall of the Roman Empire* with a luminous picture of the Roman Empire at its high point:

> In the second century of the Christian era, the empire of Rome comprehended the fairest part of the earth, and the most civilized portion of mankind. The frontiers of that extensive monarchy were guarded by ancient renown and disciplined valor. The gentle but powerful influence of laws and manners had gradually cemented the union of the provinces. Their peaceful inhabitants enjoyed and abused the advantages of wealth and luxury.[1]

---

[1]Edward Gibbon, *The History of the Decline and Fall of the Roman Empire*, ed. H. H. Milman, vol. 1 (New York: Harper & Brothers, 1850), 1.

This view of the *pax Romana*, still expressed in many introductory courses on the history of Western civilization, was not Gibbon's creation. Indeed, it is as old as Roman imperialism, which justified its own existence on the basis of the good it was doing among its subject peoples. At approximately the same time as that of the golden age which Gibbon describes, Aelius Aristides, an orator hailing from Smyrna in the province of Asia, delivered in Rome an eloquent eulogy praising Rome for all the good she was doing throughout the world:

> All localities are full of gymnasia, fountains, monumental approaches, temples, workshops, schools, and one can say that the civilized world, which had been sick from the beginning, as it were, has been brought by the right knowledge to a state of health. ... Thus like an ever-burning sacred fire the celebration never ends, but moves around from time to time and people to people, always somewhere, a demonstration justified by the way all men have fared. Thus it is right to pity those outside your hegemony, if indeed there are any, because they lose such blessings.[2]

It is not difficult to find support for such views in the monuments, both architectural and literary, of the first and second centuries of the Christian era. After all, most of

---

[2]*Roman Oration*, 24. Trans. J. H. Oliver, *The Ruling Power: A Study of the Roman Empire in the Second Century after Christ through the Roman Oration of Aelius Aristides* (Philadelphia: The American Philosophical Society, 1933).

these monuments were the product of the intellectual and economic elite, which had ample reason to rejoice in the results of Roman imperialism.

It was not only native Romans and flattering orators from Smyrna who sang the praises of Rome and her civilizing power, but also former leaders of conquered nations, such as Flavius Josephus, the turncoat Jewish rebel who received Roman citizenship and devoted his literary career to justifying Roman power and his own acquiescence to it. According to Josephus, before the rebellion "our city Jerusalem had attained greater happiness than any other city under Roman rule,"[3] and the rebellion was caused by the greed and ambition of some who sought personal gain.

Yet the very fact that the Jews did rebel, and that they had hoped to be joined by other subject peoples of the East, is an indication that not all was well within the Roman Empire. Indeed, Josephus himself indicates that one of the factors that encouraged the Jews to rebel was that there was restlessness and even rebellion in other Roman provinces, even as far away as Gaul.[4]

The much vaunted *pax Romana* was not so peaceful for many of the former inhabitants of lands conquered or otherwise annexed. What we know of the village of Philadelphia, in the region of Arsinoe in Egypt, is probably illustrative of what took place in many other areas of the empire. When Egypt became a Roman province, the village had between two and four thousand inhabitants. Rome, however, added Roman taxes on top of the traditional Egyptian taxes, thus making it very difficult for villagers to survive economi-

---

[3]*History of the Jewish War*, pref. 4.
[4]*Vita*, 37.

cally. Since those unable to pay their taxes were often tortured or sold into slavery, many resorted to flight. By Nero's time, slightly more than half a century after Egypt had become Roman, one in every eight men from Philadelphia was a tax fugitive. By the second century, two of Philadelphia's hamlets had no adult male inhabitants. By the third, the village was being resettled and bought by veterans from the Roman legions, who then employed the former inhabitants of the area as slaves or as day laborers.[5]

Economic abuse was closely connected with social and cultural discrimination. In Egypt itself, "a prime objective set by Augustus and maintained by his successors for two hundred years was to impede social mobility and keep the several population strata [Romans, Greeks, Jews, Copts] as discrete and immutable as possible."[6] According to these regulations, for instance, a Roman was forbidden to write a will in Greek; Egyptians (or Copts) who tried to "pass" as Greeks or Romans suffered the confiscation of one fourth of their property; an Egyptian woman who married a Roman and called herself Roman would be punished; etc. In short, what existed in Egypt amounted to "a veritable ancient apartheid,"[7] which manifested itself, not only in matters of property and status, but also in matters of culture, use of language, etc. In this regard, it is illuminating to realize that residents of the outlying areas of cities, normally persons of the original native population who were not allowed full citizenship by those who now ruled, were called

---

[5]Data from Nephtali Lewis, *Life in Egypt under Roman Rule* (Oxford: Clarendon, 1983), 22, 68, 164.

[6]Ibid., 32.

[7]Ibid., 34.

pároikoi—the same term employed in 1 Peter 2:11 to describe the status of Christians.

The ancient Egyptian culture and language, however, did not disappear. Many of the fugitives from villages and hamlets fled to Alexandria, where they lived and managed to survive as "undocumented aliens." Repeated edicts prohibited such fugitive Copts from living in the city, but the very reiteration of such edicts attests to their inefficacy. Others fled to the "desert"—not the sandy Sahara, but generally uninhabited lands which they began tilling and where they led a life apart from the "global" economy and empire. These "anchorites"—lit., fugitives, refugees—eventually mixed with those who had fled to the desert for religious reasons, and from this derives the religious meaning of the term "anchorite." The connection, however, is more than etymological, for the vast majority of the early Egyptian anchorites were Copts who were probably fleeing, not just the evil world, but also the evil Greco-Roman world.[8] One might say that they were "on strike" against the prevailing society and its order—and indeed, the word that was used at the time for movements of resistance among laborers, similar to today's strikes, was *anachoréseis*. It is for this reason that as late as the fourth century Athanasius, most likely himself a Copt, when persecuted by the Greco-Roman authorities, was able to find refuge among the monks of the desert. And it is also for the same reason that when the

---

[8]García M. Colombas, *El monacato primitivo*, vol. 1: *Hombres, hechos, costumbres, instituciones* (Madrid: Biblioteca de Autores Cristianos, 1974), 65-66, shows that the vast majority of the Egyptian anchorites came from the lower echelons of Coptic society, that most were illiterate and many did not know Greek, and that their ranks included thieves as well as others who would have good reason to flee from the Roman-held world.

Council of Chalcedon, under Greco-Roman direction, supported the doctrine of the "two natures" in Christ, the Coptic church opted for "monophysism."[9] Thus, the traditional picture of both Egypt and Alexandria needs to be corrected. It is true that the social elite in Alexandria spoke Greek. It is true that, with its museum and library, Alexandria supplanted Athens as the center of Greek philosophy and learning. It is also true that Greek influence in Alexandria was such that the Hebrew Bible was translated into Greek, and that learned Jews such as Philo wrote in Greek. It is even true that most long-distance transactions took place in Greek. But in spite of this superstructure of Greek language and culture, Egypt remained profoundly Egyptian, with the added factor of the many other cultures—Roman, Jewish, Syrian, Mesopotamian, Nubian—that also met and mixed there.

Perhaps we should temper our traditional understanding of Alexandria as the center of Hellenistic Greek culture with the admittedly pejorative description in a letter attributed to Emperor Hadrian and addressed to his brother-in-law Servianus, where he declares that . . .

---

[9]The case of Aba Shenute, of the White Monastery, is instructive and probably typical: "With him one can detect the growth of a self-conscious Coptic spirit growing away even linguistically from the previously dominant Greek, and which combined Monophysitism and prophecy as formidable weapons against outsiders. Shenute's work, too, of gathering in the traditional riff-raff of Egyptian society and giving its members the standing of monks and an assurance of personal salvation, as well as his passionate eloquence in his native tongue, provided the Monophysite movement in Egypt with a popular basis it never lost." W. H. C. Frend, *The Rise of the Monophysite Movement* (Cambridge University Press, 1972), 72-73.

Egypt which you so praised turns out to be flighty, vacillating, and always running after the latest fashion. There those who worship Serapis are Christians; and those who call themselves Christian bishops are devotees of Serapis. There is not a chief of a Jewish synagogue, nor a Christian elder, nor a Samaritan, who is not also a mathematician, a diviner, and a masseur for athletes.[10]

What was obvious in Alexandria was equally true in the rest of the Roman Empire: cultures were mixing at an unprecedented—and to some, alarming—rate. This was the result of two parallel phenomena: first, the resurgence of ancient cultures that had temporarily been submerged by the flood of Hellenism; second, the movement of people from one city and region to another.

Let us look first at the resurgence of ancient cultures. Although there may be some debate as to the motives behind Alexander's conquests, there is no doubt that their most enduring result was the Hellenization of the East. The far reaches of Alexander's conquests, at the very borders of India, were not as permanently impacted as the rest of his empire; but Egypt, Syria, Mesopotamia, and Asia Minor would long be connected by a common Hellenistic inheritance and by koine Greek as the lingua franca of trade and travel.

Greek culture had long been evolving in such a way that by the time of Alexander it was ready to provide the ideological framework for world conquest. The older view was that the distinction between "Greek" and "barbarian" was

---

[10]Latin text in Daniel Ruiz Bueno, ed., *Actas de los mártires* (Madrid: Biblioteca de Autores Cristianos, 1968), 252.

genetic. Barbarians were by nature inferior and incapable of the same cultural achievements as the Greeks themselves. Even in writings as late as those of Aristotle, one finds assertions to the effect that Greeks are by nature superior to barbarians.[11] But by the same time the view of Isocrates was gaining ground, that "Greek" denotes a culture rather than a parentage.[12] Clearly, the latter view was much more amenable to the Macedonian world conquerors, who themselves stood somewhere between native Greeks and "barbarians." Thus, Alexander's conquests, and their resulting attempt to Hellenize the world, were grounded in an ideology that saw Greek culture as superior to any other, and as transferable to the former "barbarians."[13]

At first, the impact of Alexander's conquests, and the Hellenizing policies of his successors in Syria and Egypt, were overwhelming. Both the Ptolemies of Egypt and the Seleucids of Syria encouraged the migration of Greek-speaking people into their territories. Many of these were soldiers who guaranteed Hellenistic rule by force of arms. Others were teachers who brought Greek letters, philosophy, and traditions; sculptors and architects who promoted Greek taste; merchants who imported Greek wares and customs. In Egypt as well as in Syria and Palestine, new cities were built after the Greek pattern. By and large, the ancient cultures and traditions seemed to have disappeared. A historian of the period describes the prevailing mood of those early years of Hellenism as follows:

---

[11]*Politics*, 1.

[12]*Panegyricus*, 50.

[13]See Moses Hadas, *Hellenistic Culture: Fusion and Diffusion* (Morningside Heights, N.Y.: Columbia University Press, 1959), 11-19.

The assimilating power of such an entity as the Hellenistic city must have been overwhelming. Partici-
pating in its institutions and ways of life, the non-
Hellenic citizens underwent rapid Hellenization,
shown most plainly in their adoption of the Greek
language: and this in spite of the fact that probably
from the beginning the non-Hellenes outnumbered
the born Greeks or Macedonians. The tremendous
subsequent growth of some of the cities, like Alexandria or Antioch, can be explained only by the contin-
ual influx of native oriental populations, which yet
did not change the Hellenistic character of the communities. Finally, in the Seleucid kingdom, in Syria
and Asia Minor, even originally oriental cities trans-
formed themselves through the adoption of Hellenic
corporate constitutions and the introduction of gym-
nasia and other typical institutions into cities of the
Greek type and received from the central government the charter granting the rights and duties of
such cities. This was a kind of refounding, evidence
of the progress of Hellenization and at the same
time a factor adding momentum to it.[14]

This was done with the acquiescence and even the en-
thusiasm of the higher classes or social elites of the conquered groups. Thus, for instance, it is clear from the story
of the Maccabees in Judea that the higher classes, especially
those contending for the high priesthood, were heavily Hellenized. Eventually, as the conflict became more focused on

---

[14]Hans Jonas, *The Gnostic Religion: The Message of the Alien God
and the Beginnings of Christianity* (Boston: Beacon Press, 1958), 7-8.

nationalistic and religious issues, the rebellion gained most of its adherents from the lower classes, urban as well as rural. In the end, however, the new Hasmonaean rulers were themselves Hellenists. Significantly, the support of the higher echelons of native societies for imperial rule continued under the Romans, as is acknowledged by Aelius Aristides:

> You [Romans] have everywhere appointed to your citizenship, or even to kinship with you, the better part of the world's talent, courage, and leadership, while the rest you recognized as a league under your hegemony.[15]

This, however, did not take place without opposition. The Maccabean revolt has already been mentioned. The Jews of Alexandria rioted and even rebelled repeatedly, notably in the year C.E. 38 and then in 115, when it took the Romans two years to quell the rebellion. Shortly before the birth of Jesus there were riots in Seleucia-on-Tigris, in which the Jews and Syrians rebelled against the politically and culturally dominant Greeks. In Egypt, under Greek rule, resistance was muted; but it erupted repeatedly after the Romans took over. In the second century (C.E. 122, 152, and 172-73) there were massive revolts. Other revolts against Rome and her power broke out in Gaul, Spain, North Africa, and elsewhere.

Such revolts were the political manifestation of the resurgence of cultures that had seemed dormant as a result of the conquests of Alexander—and later, of Rome. Hans Jonas de-

---

[15]*Roman Oration*, 59.

scribes this process by speaking of two periods within the Hellenistic age: "the period of manifest Greek dominance and oriental submersion," and "the period of reaction of a renascent East."[16] He describes the latter period as follows:

> What we do witness at the period roughly coinciding with the beginnings of Christianity is an explosion of the East. Like long-pent-up waters its forces broke through the Hellenistic crust and flooded the ancient world, flowing into the established Greek forms and filling them with their content, besides creating their own new beds.[17]

All of this was preceded by a vast literature of resistance, of which the best known is probably the biblical book of Daniel. But there were many others. In the third book of the *Sibylline Oracles*, there are Persian "prophecies" against Alexander, apparently later interpolated by a Jew wishing to make them apply to Antiochus IV.[18] Some scholars have suggested that behind the story of the book of Esther stands a Babylonian tale about the conflict between Antiochus IV and the Babylonian priests of Marduk.[19] Under Roman rule the Greeks in Egypt, although not openly rebelling, circulated clandestine writings in which resistance to Roman rule was urged and romanticized.[20]

---

[16]Jonas, *The Gnostic Religion*, 18.

[17]Ibid., 23.

[18]Samuel K. Eddy, *The King Is Dead: Studies in the Near Eastern Resistance to Hellenism*, 334-31 B.C. (Lincoln: University of Nebraska Press, 1961), 12.

[19]Ibid., 141-45.

[20]See Lewis, *Life in Egypt*, 198-200.

The resurgence of Eastern cultures, however, went far beyond resistance. It involved also a revitalization and reinterpretation of ancient culture, literature, and especially religion. The most remarkable case is the resurgence of Jewish culture under its new guise of Christianity, which soon moved beyond the confines of people of Jewish descent. The early leaders of Christianity, all Jews, reinterpreted their ancient Scriptures and turned them into a powerful instrument for the propagation of the Christian faith—and of much of Jewish culture and tradition with it. Even earlier, Judaism itself had begun to make inroads among Gentiles, gaining numerous proselytes as well as "God-fearers." Something similar happened in the case of the ancient religious traditions of Pharaonic Egypt. The myth of Isis and Osiris and the afterlife it promised, formerly limited to the Egyptian aristocracy, now became available to any who would believe.[21] Likewise, Attis and Cybele left their ancient Eastern home and invaded the Roman aristocracy.[22]

This resurgence, and its impact on distant places, was possible in part because of the second dominant phenomenon of the age, the mobility of people from city to city, and from region to region. War, trade, and civil unrest had long uprooted people from their ancestral homes. The dispersion of Judaism, and the large numbers of Jews living in Alexandria, Asia Minor, Mesopotamia, and Rome, are well known.

[21]See Jean Leclant, *Inventoire bibliographique des Isiaca: Répertoire analytique des travaux relatifs à la difussion des cultes Isiaques* (Leiden: Brill, 1972). Of particular interest, and not included in the former, is Sharon Kelly Hoyob, *The Cult of Isis among Women in the Graeco-Roman World* (Leiden: Brill, 1975).

[22]See Maarten J. Vermaseren, *The Legend of Attis in Greek and Roman Art* (Leiden: Brill, 1966).

It suffices to read the New Testament book of Acts to see that there were Jewish synagogues in most major cities in Asia Minor. Babylonian astrologers, Persian traders, and Phrygian slaves were a common sight in Alexandria. The early readers of the Gospel of Matthew knew what Persian magi were. Egyptian merchants traveling to Rome brought the myth of Isis and Osiris; and others, probably from Phrygia, brought the myth of Attis and Cybele. The comment of Tacitus is well known, that his beloved Rome had become "that cesspool for all that is base and sordid from every corner of the earth."[23] What was happening in Rome was also taking place in every other region of the Roman Empire, particularly in those cities and areas whose prosperity attracted merchants, artisans, slaves, and charlatans.

Significantly, not all Romans felt the same way about the influx of Eastern cultures and religions. While most aristocrats deplored the threat of base "superstitions" such as Christianity,[24] many joined what were deemed to be more respectable cults, and the majority of the cultured adopted much of Greek philosophy and even language.

Thus, in the first century the Mediterranean basin was a cosmopolitan environment in which all cultures and traditions were at home, and in which most were equally alien. A

---

[23]*Annals*, 15.44.

[24]Marcus Aurelius, *Meditations*, 11.3, says that the soul should be ready to be separated from the body at any time, but not out of "sheer obstinacy, as is the case with Christians." Galen declares that, although Christians act in the same way as philosophers, in order to lead the philosophical life they are not guided by rational arguments, which they are incapable of following, but instead need parables and miracles. See Robert L. Wilken, *The Christians as the Romans Saw Them* (New Haven: Yale University Press, 1984), 77-83.

Jew from Jerusalem wishing to go to sea probably would go to Caesarea, a typically pagan city built by Herod the Great and named in honor of Augustus Caesar. Even in Palestine, that Jew would not have felt quite at home. And in Rome, that same Jew would have been able to find a synagogue to make him feel somewhat at home. Likewise, a Roman crossing the Subura on his way from the Esquiline to the Forum would probably have heard Greek, Aramaic, and Punic, as well as a number of Germanic tongues, and would not have felt quite at home. And yet, that same Roman would not have felt quite away from home in Caesarea in Palestine or even in distant Spain.

In Asia Minor, the region which most interests us here, the situation was similar, yet different. There, the encounter with Greek culture had begun long before the conquests of Alexander. Indeed, the coast of Asia Minor, known to the Greeks as Ionia, had long been considered part of Greece. Ephesus, its main city, was both fully Greek and fully Eastern. According to Greek tradition, the Greek city was founded by Androclus, the son of the king of Athens, in 1087 B.C.E. Its mixed origin may be seen in its most famous object of worship, apparently a meteorite (see Acts 19:35), which was eventually identified with the Greek Artemis. As soon as one moved inland, the rugged terrain divided the region into several independent kingdoms, which few conquerors since the Hittites had been able to unify and hold. Hittites, Cimmerians, Phrygians, Lydians, and many others shared the cultural landscape. Thus, in contrast to Egypt, Syria, or Persia, there was no unified culture to offer long-term resistance to Hellenism. Indeed, some seem to have welcomed the Macedonian conquest. Sardis, for instance, boasted much of Greek culture and architecture a hundred fifty years before Alexander. When Alexander's army approached, we are told that the leaders of Sardis, and even some Persian commanders, welcomed him as a liberator from the Persian yoke. From that point on, in spite of many political vicissitudes, Sardis remained a Greek city.

As the Macedonian empire broke down, the region once again divided into several independent kingdoms— Pontos, Bithynia, Pisidia, Cappadocia, etc. Many of the rulers of these kingdoms were related to each other and to various Hellenistic dynasties, and therefore promoted Hellenism among their followers, especially the elite. On the surface at least, Asia Minor was thoroughly Hellenized, and there was little resistance to Greek culture.

Yet even here not all was well. In 90 B.C.E. there were major uprisings of the rural proletariat in the central and western regions of the Anatolian peninsula. We know from Acts 14:11 that even in a city such as Lystra the populace still spoke the Lycaonian language. One wonders whether there is a connection between ignorance of the Greek language and the economic oppression leading to revolt.

At any rate, if there was no major opposition to the Hellenization of the region, there certainly was much resistance to its Romanization. Although by the time John wrote Revelation Pergamum had become a center of Roman power, two hundred years earlier, when King Attalos III of Pergamum bequeathed his kingdom to Rome, resistance was fierce. Led by Aristonicos, and apparently inspired by revolutionary notions coming from Rome itself,[25] the slaves and urban poor,

---

[25]Blossios of Cumai, who had been an advisor of the Gracchi in Rome, was also among the advisors and supporters of Aristonicos. See Eddy, *The King Is Dead*, 177-78.

as well as many in the countryside, joined in rebellion and had to be forcefully crushed by Roman might. Early in the first century B.C.E., the ancient *Oracle of Hystaspes*, of Persian origin and originally written to resist Hellenization, was reinterpreted to support Phrygian resistance to Roman invasion. Apparently to resist the Roman conquest of Pontos, the *Sibylline Oracles* were interpolated with words that sound much like those of the Apocalypse of John:

> For all the wealth that Rome took from tribute-
>   paying Asia,
> Three times as much Asia shall take back from
>   Rome,
> And shall repay her for her deadly arrogance.
> And for those Asians enslaved in Italian homes,
> Twenty times as many Italians shall toil for Asia
> In poverty, and shall be held for debts a thousand-
>   fold.[26]

In summary, one could conclude that...

> It is a notable fact that the region could show no indigenous program of hostility to Hellenism; nonetheless, it was important as the place where anti-Hellenic prophecy came to be turned against Rome.[27]

It is significant that John's Apocalypse may be seen as part of this tradition of resistance to Roman rule. Besides the well-known description in chapter 17 of Rome as the

---

[26]*Sibylline Oracles*, 3.350-55. Quoted in Eddy, *The King Is Dead*, 179, n. 32.

[27]Ibid., 182.

Great Whore sitting on seven mountains (to which we shall return), two other less noted passages should be mentioned in this regard.

The first of these is the opening of the second seal and the emergence of the second horseman, in Revelation 6:3-4. This second horseman, according to John, "was permitted to take peace from the earth, so that people would slaughter one another; and he was given a great sword." This "great sword" (*máchaira*) is technically different from the battle sword (*romphaía*) carried by soldiers. It is actually the executioner's sword, a symbol of power and authority. This sword was the symbol of imperial authority, whose right to inflict the death penalty was called "the right of the sword" (*máchaira*). It was also the symbol of imperial authority bestowed on provincial governors. It is the "sword" to which Paul refers in Romans 13:4: "the authority does not bear the sword (*máchaira*) in vain." In conclusion...

...after the first rider made original readers of this book think of Parthia and foreign invasion, they would see in the second rider a symbol of Rome and its power.

Ironically, Rome boasted of having brought peace to the lands it had conquered—the *pax romana*. This is partially true. But it is also true that many of the conquered people were recruited as Roman auxiliaries to fight against their former neighbors. Constant rebellions plagued the Empire. For many of the conquered peoples, the much-vaunted Roman peace was the peace of death. It is also clear that John the Seer had neither love nor admiration for the Roman Empire. Thus, in an ironic twist of the Roman claim to have brought peace, John says that this rider "was permitted to take peace from the earth, so that people would slaughter one another."[28]

The second such passage is Revelation 13:1-10, where "the beast from the sea" appears. Although a number of commentators have ascribed various meanings to this particular beast, it should suffice to point out that, from the point of view of Asia Minor, Rome and all the symbols of its power—governors, decrees, tax collectors—came from the sea. The beast from the sea is none other than Roman might, come to "make war on the saints" while "all the inhabitants of the earth...worship it."

Thus, the book of Revelation is set in, and is part of, a situation in which there was much cultural and political conflict, even though often hidden under the mantle of the *pax Romana*. In order to understand the book of Revelation, it must be placed within that context.

---

[28]Catherine Gunsalus González and Justo L. González, *Revelation* (Louisville: Westminster/John Knox Press, 1997), 48.

III

Culture and Conflict
in the Early Church

The early church had no problem with garlic. Indeed, garlic was and has remained a constant and practically universal feature of the Near East, sometimes to the disgust of others. Thus, early in the twentieth century, a professor at the American College in Beirut wrote about garlic:

> It is now, as in the days of the ancient Egyptians, a favourite addition to the complex stews and the roasts of the Orientals. It is cultivated everywhere in the East. Too often the natives reek with its stale, penetrating odour.[1]

But if the early church did not have a problem with garlic, it did have significant problems as it crossed from one culture to another. Too often we glibly quote Paul's declaration to the Corinthians, as if it were an easy matter:

---

[1]George E. Post, in *A Dictionary of the Bible*, ed. James Hastings (New York: Charles Scribner's Sons, 1902), 2: 110.

To the Jews I became as a Jew, in order to win Jews. To those under the law I became as one under the law (though I myself am not under the law) so that I might win those under the law. To those outside the law I became as one outside the law (though I am not free from God's law but am under Christ's law) so that I might win those outside the law. To the weak I became weak, so that I might win the weak. I have become all things to all people, that I might by all means save some. I do it all for the sake of the gospel, so that I may share in its blessings. (1 Cor 9:20-23)

This is a very significant and beautiful passage about communication through solidarity, or perhaps about what missiologists call "accommodation." It is about the type of mission that will eventually bring about a multicultural church. But it is also a passage of struggle and confrontation. The context is important. In chapter 8, Paul is dealing with the question of food sacrificed to idols—a multicultural question if there ever was one! Christians know that idols do not really exist, and therefore there is nothing particularly evil about the food that has been sacrificed to them and is now available for sale. But Paul goes on to speak of those who do not have this understanding, those who "have become so accustomed to idols until now, they think of the food they eat as food offered to an idol; and their conscience, being weak, is defiled" (8:7). Paul is clear that this is a matter of tradition, culture, and depth of understanding. In truth, "food will not bring us close to God. We are no worse off if we do not eat, and no better off if we do" (8:8). Today we would say that it is a cultural issue. In the sixteenth century, Lutheran theologians would have called it *adiaphora*. In principle, one can be equally faithful by abstaining from such meat as by consuming it. But that is not the whole picture. Paul reminds us of the conscience of the weak, who may see good Christians eating meat sacrificed to the idols and conclude that the idols do exist and have power. Such a person, misled by an erroneous interpretation of one's exercise of freedom, may be "destroyed" (8:11). In that case, what would otherwise be a matter of freedom becomes one of obedience, because "when you thus sin against members of your family, and wound their conscience when it is weak, you sin against Christ" (8:12).

Paul then goes on to assert his freedom to eat or not to eat, even though "if food is a cause of their falling, I will never eat meat, so that I may not cause one of them to fall" (8:13). It is for this freedom in subjection that he is then arguing in chapter 9, which begins with the phrase, "Am I not free?" This freedom, as a matter of principle, would allow him to eat and drink, to take a wife with him as he travels, and to live off his preaching. Others do this, and it is their right, just as it is his. But he has decided not to exercise this right for the same reason he has decided not to eat food sacrificed to idols, that is, the effectiveness of his witness and his teaching among persons who would not otherwise understand. In conclusion, says Paul, "though I am free with respect to all, I have made myself a slave to all, so that I might win more of them" (9:19). It is as a conclusion to this argument that Paul declares that he has adjusted to various groups of people, becoming like them in order to win some of them.

What all of this means is that Paul is not simply making minor adjustments in his behavior. He is aware of serious cultural differences among those whom he is trying to evangelize. He knows that these differences are not central to the gospel. But he also knows that unless he takes them into account he cannot be an effective and obedient apostle of Jesus Christ. These issues come to the foreground at various points in the New Testament. Most prominent among them is Paul's epistle to the Galatians, where he says that he rebuked Peter for changing his attitude about eating with Gentiles:

> I opposed him to his face, because he stood self-condemned; for until certain people came from James, he used to eat with the Gentiles. But after they came, he drew back and kept himself separate for fear of the circumcision faction.... But when I saw that they were not acting consistently with the truth of the gospel, I said to Cephas before them all, "If you, though a Jew, live like a Gentile and not like a Jew, how can you compel the Gentiles to live like Jews?" (Gal 2:11b-12, 14)

There are many aspects of this passage that are not altogether clear and are still the subject of debate among scholars. Yet, one thing is clear: Paul does not believe that simple "accommodation" is enough! It does not suffice to say, "in Rome, do as the Romans do"—or among the Gentiles and the Christian Jews of Antioch do as the Gentiles do, but when James and others come from Jerusalem, do as they expect you to do. Nor is it a matter of applying a series of universal practices set by the center for the periphery—in which case the issue would have been "resolved" quite simply: Gentile converts to Christianity have to be circumcised and keep the dietary as well as all the other laws of Israel. It is a much more complex matter in which what is most important is to "walk straight" (the NRSV translates this as "acting consistently") in the truth of the gospel. This truth is one of unity, and therefore Paul cannot tolerate an "accommodation" that in fact avoids the issue by separating the Gentile Christian community from its Jewish counterpart.

As we turn from the epistles of Paul to the book of Acts, we find that the issue of culture and language appears practically at the very beginning of the book, where Parthians, Medes, Elamites, and residents of Mesopotamia, Judea, Cappadocia, and so on are all made to hear of the mighty deeds of God, each in their own tongue. In this particular passage, it is important to note that all these people are *not* given the power to understand the language of Peter and his companions. Rather, they are made to understand "each in their own language." At Pentecost, God confirms the translatability of the gospel, which does not have to be heard in the language of the apostles to be authentic. If catholicity is understood as outlined in chapter 1 of this book, only a translatable and constantly translated gospel can be catholic.

We know—and we shall see in a moment—that there was in Palestinian Judaism considerable tension between those who spoke Aramaic (which they called "Hebrew") and those Jews from the Diaspora who had returned to Palestine but were not native speakers of Aramaic. These language differences most likely stood for many other differences in costume, behavior, diet, etc. In today's language, one could say that there was an "Aramaic-only movement" in first-century Palestine. In that case, Pentecost is God's radical and final NO to such a movement. The manner in which the Spirit works is *not* by making all the various peo-

ple of the world understand the language of the Twelve, but
rather by making it possible for them to hear each language
group in its own tongue. This is of enormous significance
for the life and mission of the church, as missiologist Lamin
Sanneh has pointed out:

> The gospel demands a plural frontier for its diffu-
> sion, looking with alarm at the notion of a hermeti-
> cally sealed culture as the exclusive conveyance of
> God's truth...no one culture can be God's favorite.
> The result is pluralism on a radical scale, one that
> even institutional Christianity finds difficult to ac-
> cept or promote. But if translatability is the taproot
> of Christian expansion, then resistance to it by ec-
> clesiastical institutions is like the rebellion of the
> branches against the tree...
>
> Thus mission as translation makes the bold, fun-
> damental assertion that the recipient culture is the
> authentic destination of God's salvific promise and,
> as a consequence, has an honored place under the
> "kindness of God," with the attendant safeguards
> against cultural absolutism.[2]

It would be possible—and could well be the subject of
another book—to read the entire book of Acts following this
theme of translation, cultural conflict, and resolution and
the multiple conversions of the church and the apostles as
they discover new dimensions to their mission. For our purposes here, a few highlights will have to suffice.

---

[2]Lamin Sanneh, *Translating the Message: The Missionary Impact on
Culture* (Maryknoll, N.Y.: Orbis Books, 1989), 30-31.

In Acts 6, we are told that "the Hellenists complained against the Hebrews because their widows were being neglected in the daily distribution." It is important to understand that all these people are Jewish Christians. Those whom the text calls "Hebrews" are in reality Aramaic-speaking Jews, people from Jerusalem and the surrounding area. Those whom the text calls "Hellenists" are also Jews. But they have become much more Hellenized than their "Hebrew" counterparts. Most likely, they grew up away from Palestine, and they speak Greek much more fluently than Aramaic. The Aramaic-speaking Jewish Christians are the leaders in the church. That is not surprising: they are the natives of the area (although they are also Galileans, and as such are marginalized by the "in" crowd in Jerusalem, as the gospel and the early chapters of Acts have made abundantly clear). They are the inheritors of the original proclamation of the gospel. The Greek-speakers are the newcomers.

The result of all this is that the Greek-speaking portion of the congregation is somewhat marginal within the Jerusalem church—and also within the religious structure of the city as a whole. Their widows do not feel they are being fairly treated in receiving support from the whole congregation. And they are probably right.

There is complaining. And the complaining is against the leadership, against the Twelve. Indeed, a few verses earlier Luke has told us that those who sold properties and brought the proceeds for the relief of the needy "laid them at the apostles' feet." The apostles were responsible for the management of resources, and if there was criticism, it was ultimately directed at them.

So, what do they do? They call a meeting of the whole congregation. They do not downgrade the problem. Today some would say that the problem is that some widows do not know their place. We have already given them something. Something is better than nothing. Let them be quiet and take what is given to them, or go away and leave us alone. Today we would speak of "the problem of the widows," or the "problem" of one ethnic minority or another. But the fact is that, if one reads the book of Acts as a whole, it is clear that the widows were not the problem. The problem was the Holy Spirit, who on that day of Pentecost was poured on all flesh, young and old, sons and daughters, and invited all to join, "Parthians and Medes and Elamites and residents of Mesopotamia, Judea and Cappadocia, Pontus and Asia, Phrygia and Pamphilia, Egypt and the parts of Libya belonging to Cyrene, and visitors from Rome, both Jews and proselytes, Cretans and Arabians."

The problem is not caused by the widows, or by the Hellenists, or by any ethnic minority. The problem is caused by that subversive Spirit of God, who bloweth from where the Spirit listeth, and who destroys all our neat patterns and classifications. And, because the problem was caused by the Spirit, the leadership took it seriously and decided something needed to be done. (Note also that the reason that moved them to action was the fact that there was "complaining." They did not try to ignore the complaints of those who felt left out. They did not wait until somebody began picketing the church, or even until a caucus was formed!)

The "something" to be done would involve a new administrative structure. The Twelve decide that they have the charge to proclaim the gospel—evidently largely in Aramaic—and cannot in good conscience spend the time organizing the relief work for the widows. (Apparently the Holy Spirit does not agree with this division of labor, for the first thing we are told, immediately after the election of the seven, is that one of them preached, not just any sermon, but the longest sermon in the entire book of Acts!)

So, the leadership suggests that the congregation is to choose seven from among its members to carry out such tasks. Today we have a solution for this kind of "problem." If we are slightly enlightened, we appoint a token member of the excluded group to serve on the committee dealing with the distribution of resources. If we are a little more enlightened, we set up a quota for such tokens. If we are still more enlightened, we allow those minority representatives to administer that part of *our* resources that *we* have set aside for them. But that is not what this congregation does. Those who are chosen all have Greek names. Some might be natives, but chances are most are not. At least one is listed as a proselyte from Antioch—a Gentile who had become a Jew. So this congregation, where presumably the majority are still Aramaic-speaking, and where evidently the Aramaic-speaking still hold power—that was the reason for the "complaining" in the first place—chooses leadership that empowers those who had been more marginal.

Given the political situation, empowering the Greek-speaking segment of the congregation may well have been a courageous thing to do. It implied a sharing of leadership with a new part of the community. It gave leadership to those who might raise even more questions about the church in the wider city. It would lead to strife and conflict that might possibly have been avoided had the apostles refused to expand the leadership beyond their own small group. (We know that it did give rise to strife and conflict, for in the very next chapter of Acts persecution breaks out against the church. It breaks out first of all against the Hellenistic Jews, such as Stephen, who have become Christians. And, if one reads the story carefully, one notes that for the first time in the book of Acts the enemies of Christianity are able to gain the support of the people and to join their efforts with those of the high priests, the scribes, and the elders, in order to suppress Christianity.)

In Acts 10, we have a story that is often called "the conversion of Cornelius," when in fact it is just as much the conversion of Peter. Once again, cultural issues are at stake. Peter makes this quite clear when he tells Cornelius and his companions: "You yourselves know that it is unlawful for a Jew to associate with or to visit a Gentile; but God has shown me that I should not call anyone profane or unclean" (Acts 10:28)—in other words, if it were up to me, that is precisely what I would call you! In the end, however, Peter himself is converted, coming to a broader understanding of the gospel and its reach: "I truly understand that God shows no partiality, but in every nation anyone who fears him and does what is right is acceptable to him" (10:34). In the next chapter, after the church in Jerusalem calls Peter to account, it too is converted: "Then God has given even to Gentiles the repentance that leads to life" (11:18).

Finally, this rapid survey of cultural issues and conflicts in the early life of the church as depicted in Acts must include some consideration of Acts 15—the so-called Council of Jerusalem. Clearly, this gathering had to do with the issues raised by the addition of Gentiles to the church. Significantly, the conflict was initiated in Antioch, when "certain individuals came down from Judea and were teaching the brothers, 'Unless you are circumcised according to the custom of Moses, you cannot be saved'" (Acts 15:1). In other words, there are those from the center who are disturbed because those from the periphery are being admitted without sufficient adjustment to the center. The "Council" then takes place, and issues a "decree" whose exact purpose bears some examination.

There are some significant variants in the text of the "decree." The most ancient extant text (the Chester Beatty papyrus) lists only three things from which converts must abstain: what has been sacrificed to idols, what is strangled, and blood. The so-called Egyptian text, which most scholars believe to be the most ancient, and which is attested by a variety of manuscripts, adds fornication to the list. Finally, the Western text, apparently of slightly later date, omits that which is strangled and adds a negative version of the golden rule: "Do not do unto others what you do not wish to have them do unto you." Thus, the Western text implies that the prohibitions are essentially moral in character, while the earlier texts appear to emphasize ritual matters. For instance, what is meant by abstaining from "blood"? If, as is the case in the Western text, "what is strangled" is omitted, abstaining from blood takes on the meaning of not killing or committing violence. Indeed, it was thus that the Western church came to interpret the apostolic decree, turning it into the basis for its listing of the three great (some would say, unforgivable) sins: homicide, idolatry, and fornication. If, on the other hand, "blood" appears next to "what is strangled," it is clear that this has to do with the ancient prohibition in Jewish law against eating blood, or even the meat of animals that have not been properly bled. One might even go further, and claim that the prohibition of eating "what has been sacrificed to idols" is somehow related to the improper slaughtering of the animals, and not just to their connection with idolatry. In fact, the four prohibitions listed are a summary of what according to the Law of Moses was to be expected of every foreigner living in Israel (Lev 17:8–18:30), as well as of the Israelites themselves. The traditional interpretations of these texts and depictions of events usually run along one of two lines. The most common line of interpretation is that the Council of Jerusalem was determining the minimum elements of the Law that Gentiles had to obey in order to become Christians—or, in other words, how much of the Law was still valid for Christians. This is obviously a question that comes to the foreground as the church ceases being mostly a Jewish community and becomes almost exclusively Gentile in origin. That, however, was still not the case at the time of the purported Council of Jerusalem or at the time of the writing of Acts. A second line of interpretation is that the number of Gentiles in the church was growing rapidly, and therefore the church had to deal with the question of communion between Christian Jews and Gentiles. There was traditionally a list of minimum requirements that Gentiles living in Israel had to obey, and now these were transferred to the Gentiles who wished to join a community composed mainly of Jewish Christians. If so, what we have here is a prime example of cross-cultural negotiation, even though all the participants in the actual conversation in Jerusalem are themselves Jews—something similar to the Administrative Board of my friend's church, composed mostly of garlic haters, establishing a list of fairly liberal guidelines within which the garlic lovers may share the same space.

The situation, however, appears to have been much more complex. Scholars are beginning to question the traditional view, that most Jews rejected Christianity, and that therefore most early Christian growth was among Gentiles.

Indeed, it may be argued that for many Jews from the Diaspora Christianity had the same sort of appeal that Reformed Judaism has had for many Jews in the liberal, bourgeois North-Atlantic. Christianity was a way of retaining their Jewish roots while opening further to the surrounding culture and society.

> For Hellenized Jews who had social and intellectual problems with the Law, the God-Fearers could easily have been a tempting model of an alternative, fully Greek Judaism.... But the God-Fearers were not a movement. The Christians were.
>
> When the Apostolic Council decided not to require converts to observe the Law, they created a religion free of ethnicity. Tradition has it that the first fruits of this break with the Law was the rapid success of the mission to the Gentiles. But who would have been the first to hear of the break? Who would have had the greatest initial benefits from it? ...
>
> Christianity offered twice as much cultural continuity to the Hellenized Jews as to Gentiles. If we examine the marginality of the Hellenized Jews, torn between two cultures, we may note how Christianity offered to retain much of the religious content of *both* cultures and to resolve the contradictions between them.[3]

If this interpretation is correct, what actually happened in the early church was not that all or even the vast majority of

---

[3]Rodney Stark, *The Rise of Christianity: A Sociologist Reconsiders History* (Princeton: Princeton University Press, 1996), 58-59.

Jews rejected Christianity. It was rather that many Jews did become Christians, and this in turn led to two reactions whose consequences are abundantly attested to in later history. First, on the part of the more traditional Jews, there was a movement to consolidate the faith around the institution of the synagogue, in order to avoid further "defections" to the sect of the Galileans. Second, there was a corresponding movement among Christians—and in particular Christian leaders who saw themselves as guardians of orthodoxy—to counteract the "Judaizing" influence, not of traditional Jews or of the synagogue itself, but of the fairly large contingent of Jews within the church. On the basis of this interpretation of events, it has been suggested that much of our reading of early Christian-Jewish relations has to be revised. For instance, "rather than dismiss Chrysostom as merely a raving bigot or as an unscrupulous manipulator of Jewish scapegoats, why not see him as an early leader in the movement to *separate* a church and synagogue that were greatly entwined?"[4]

What all of this means is that from the very outset Christianity existed at the edge of cultures, so to speak. Within the very Judaism in which it was born, it soon appealed mostly to Hellenistic Jews, marginalized both by the more traditional Jews and by the more sophisticated elements within Hellenism. Within the early Christian community itself, there were cultural conflicts from the very beginning. Its most prominent leaders had more than one name, reflecting various cultural settings: Paul/Saul, Simon/Simeon/Cephas/Peter. And yet, rather than shying away from intercultural conflict, Christianity thrived precisely at those edges where conflict was inevitable.

---

[4]Ibid., 66.

IV

John of Patmos
in His Cultural Setting

There is not much that can be said about the author of the book of Revelation. Three times at the beginning of the book (1:1, 4, 9), and once again toward the end (22:8), he tells us that his name is John. On two of those occasions, slightly more is said about him: he is a "servant" of Jesus Christ (1:1), and a "brother" of his readers (1:9). But these titles are sufficiently commonplace among Christians not to tell us anything about him. He adds that he shares with his readers in "the persecution and the kingdom and the patient endurance," that he is on the island of Patmos "because of the word of God and the testimony of Jesus," and that his vision (or at least part of it) took place "on the Lord's day" (1:9-10). Beyond this, the book says little about its author.

Very soon Christian tradition began identifying this "John" with the apostle of the same name. Toward the middle of the second century, some fifty or sixty years after the book was written, Justin Martyr already took this as a fact:

"There was among us a certain man whose name was John, one of the apostles of Christ, who prophesied through a revelation (*en apokalypsei*) that those who believe in our Christ will dwell a thousand years in Jerusalem, and that this will be followed by the universal resurrection . . ."[1] Scarcely three decades later, Irenaeus took for granted that his teacher Polycarp had sat at the feet of John the Apostle, who had lived at Ephesus until the time of Trajan (early second century).[2] Thus, John of Patmos, the prophet whose connections with Ephesus and with the entire province of Asia are obvious in his book, became identified with John the Apostle. This view was upheld by the Muratorian Canon, by Clement of Alexandria,[3] by Tertullian,[4] and eventually by mainstream Christian tradition—although there were always some who did not accept this identification.

Both the identification of John of Patmos with the apostle John and the rejection of that identification, however, were based on ulterior purposes. Most of those who claimed that the two Johns were the same were seeking to bolster the authority of a book that was not always well received. When Irenaeus declared that John the Apostle had lived in Ephesus for a long time, he was using this supposed fact to undergird the apostolic authority of John's successors as bishops of Ephesus.[5] Likewise, those who denied that

---

[1] *Dialogue with Trypho*, 81.4.

[2] *Adv. haer.*, 3.4.

[3] *Quis dives salvetur*, 42.

[4] *Adv. Marc.*, 3.14.

[5] *Adv. haer.*, 3.3: "Then, again, the Church in Ephesus, founded by Paul, and having John remaining among them permanently until the times of Trajan, is a true witness of the tradition of the apostles." (ANF, 1:416). Cf. *Adv. haer.* 2.22.

Revelation was written by the apostle John did so because
they did not like its theology. The first whose name has
been preserved was a Roman priest by the name of Gaius,
who apparently was disturbed that the Montanists used the
book of Revelation as an authority on which to base their
doctrines, and who therefore simply declared that Revelation was written not by John, but by the archheretic Ce-
rinthus.[6] After the conversion of Constantine, there was
general opposition to the book of Revelation, supposedly
because it was not written by an apostle, but in fact because
its words about the Roman Empire were too harsh for Con-
stantinian ears.

The fact is that we know very little about the identity or
the life of John of Patmos. Even the assertion that he was
on the island of Patmos as an exile because of religious persecution is not absolutely certain. He does say that he was
on Patmos "because of the word of God and the testimony
of Jesus" (1:9). Traditionally, this has been understood as indicating that he had been sent there by the Roman authorities. That is probably true, but the text could also be understood as declaring simply that he had gone to Patmos to
preach.

On the other hand, although the book of Revelation
says very little about John, it does *tell* us more. It tells us,
first of all, that he was a Jew, deeply immersed in the culture and traditions of his people. Indeed, there is no book in
the entire New Testament that has more allusions to the
Hebrew Scriptures or to other books of Jewish origin. These
allusions are so frequent that one would be hard pressed to
find many verses in Revelation without at least one of them;

---

[6]As reported by Irenaeus, *Adv. haer.*, 3.28.

and in some verses there are several, sometimes intertwined in such a way that it is difficult to separate them. (At this point I am reminded of the sermons of John Wesley, in which almost every sentence includes an allusion to the King James Bible. As one reads Wesley's sermons, it appears that most of these allusions are not even conscious. He was so steeped in that particular version of the Bible, it had so shaped his language and his thought, that when he spoke on certain topics allusions to that version came out almost unbidden. I suspect that if our knowledge of the Jewish literature circulating in the first century were as complete as our knowledge of the King James Bible, we would discover even more allusions to that literature in the book of Revelation.)

The sources of these allusions are multiple. Clearly, one of John's favorite sources is the book of Daniel. Many of the beasts that he sees are patterned after similar creatures in Daniel. As we shall see, the very phrase "out of every tribe and nation," which is at the heart of this book, is drawn from Daniel. Much of the symbolism in Revelation cannot be understood apart from its earlier use in Daniel. Allusions to Ezekiel are also frequent, as well as to several other books of the Hebrew Bible. Also, there are many points of affinity between various passages and phrases in Revelation and much of the Jewish literature of the time—1 Enoch, 4 Ezra, the Apocalypse of Abraham, 2 Baruch, perhaps some of the sources of the Testaments of the Twelve Patriarchs, etc. The problem is that, since John never quotes a text verbatim, but rather alludes to it by using its words, style, and imagery, it is very difficult to know whether he had actually read a particular text or was simply reflecting a source or tradition common to him and to that other text. To complicate matters, some of these Jewish texts are difficult to date, and therefore it is not certain that they existed when John wrote his book.

Significantly, although the other authors of the New Testament quote the Hebrew Bible from the Septuagint, John does not seem to be aware of that Greek translation—or at least does not use it. His references to the Hebrew Bible—which are never extensive quotations, but rather allusions—seem to be his own translation, quoted from memory. His Greek is not as polished as that of Paul or other New Testament writers. It is full of Hebraisms, and sometimes his grammatical constructions appear awkward or unorthodox.

At any rate, one thing is clear: John of Patmos was deeply steeped in his Jewish culture and tradition. Most scholars stress his connection with Palestinian Judaism. This connection is so strong that it has even been suggested—although not generally accepted—that the book is the work of the community gathered around John the Baptist, to which Christians later added the specific references to Christ.[7] While such a hypothesis presumes too much, the evidence for John's connection with Palestinian Judaism is impressive. Even the most sober conclusion as to who John was affirms that connection:

> The best we may claim is that the author of Revelation is an otherwise unknown Christian prophet, likely an itinerant prophet, and, probably, a Pales-

---

[7] J. Massyngberde Ford, *Revelation: A New Translation, with Introduction and Commentary*, vol. 38 of *The Anchor Bible* (New York: Doubleday, 1975). Ford claims that chapters 4–11 reflect the original community of the Baptist, and chapters 12-22 reflect later developments within that community. Christian additions are the first three chapters and some interpolation in chapter 22.

tinian by birth. Not very impressive, it might seem.
Yet, it is rather more than can be said of the authors
of many other biblical writings.[8]

There is more, however, that can be said about John of
Patmos, particularly when one reads his book from the perspective of the cultural conflicts of our time. John is a Palestinian Jew living in Asia Minor. His very use of the Greek
language reflects that background—as my own use of the
English language reflects that I am a Cuban living in the
United States. Just as Paul-Saul and Simon-Cephas-Peter
lived at the border between cultures, and moved from one
side of that border to the other, so did John the Palestinian
Jew live in Asia Minor. The very fact that he did not use the
Septuagint, but apparently translated from his own recollec-
tion of the Hebrew text, indicates that his very writing was
an exercise in such crossing—much as I, when addressing
an English-speaking public, often find myself translating
into English a biblical text that I can recall only in Spanish.

Among Hispanics in the United States, this experience
is often expressed in terms of "mestizaje." A "mestizo" is a
person of mixed breed—what those who claim racial or ethnic purity would call a "mongrel." The mestizo has two lines
of parentage, two possible sources of identity, and does not
really fit in either. The mestizo is a hyphenated person:
Mexican-American, Hispanic-American, Cuban-American.
The mestizo is at home in two places, and is not quite at
home in either. The hyphen itself seems to indicate that
there is an irresoluble difference and tension between these

---

[8]Wilfrid J. Harrington, *Revelation*, vol. 16 of *Sacra Pagina* (Col-
legeville: The Liturgical Press, 1993), 9.

two identities, and that the tension exists within the very being of the mestizo. As a result, neither of the two poles of the mestizo's identity fully accepts him or her; there is always the other pole, which seems to justify exclusion. In Texas, the Mexican-American is *Mexican*-American; in Mexico, the same person is Mexican-*American*.

John is a Palestinian Jew (one of those whom Acts 6 would call "Hebrews") living in Asia Minor who has embraced a Jewish sect that is making headway among Hellenistic Jews and among Gentile God-fearers. He is proud of his Jewish heritage, in which he is deeply steeped. He is used to thinking and speaking as a Jew, to the point that phrases from Jewish tradition and ritual constantly flow from his pen.

John, however, writes his book in Greek. Why? He is, after all, part of a community that is also mostly Jewish. There certainly must have been enough Jews in the churches of Asia to explain to others some of John's constant references to Daniel, to Ezekiel, and in general to Hebrew tradition and literature. That community, however, is also in a mestizo situation, and that is why John's book is in Greek.

Here again, the mestizo and the immigrant situation in this country helps us understand John's position amid the cultures of his time. I have written a number of books about Hispanic theology, to be used mostly by Hispanics in this country; and I have written them in English. I have done so because, if I hope to be read by the younger generation of Hispanics in the United States I must write in English. That is not to say that my prospective readers do not know Spanish; they do, and most of them are proud to speak it. The situation is much more complex. First of all, although they speak Spanish, they have never studied in Spanish, and therefore their reading facility is greater in English. Second, since they must function in an English-speaking environment, material written in English is more readily and directly applicable to that environment. Finally, and sadly, since most of their school books are in English, many of them have subconsciously come to identify the English language with academic respectability and authority.

John writes in Greek because that is the language that all in his congregations will understand, even though he himself is ill at ease in that language, and clearly is more at home in Aramaic. He expects his book to be read aloud in the congregations he is addressing. At the beginning of his book, he says: "Blessed is the one who reads aloud the words of the prophecy, and blessed are those who hear" (Rev 1:3). Therefore, he writes in the lingua franca of the region, in the language of the dominant culture, even though this means that both he and many of the hearers of his book will have to write and to hear in a language that is not strictly their own. This would be true, not only of Jews in the congregations, but also of Lycaoneans, Phrygians, and others. In a multicultural setting, the language of the dominant culture is used by others as a means of communication—much as pan-African conferences today are conducted in English and French.

John's Greek is not very good by the standards of the time. At points it is even awkward—as is my English when I cannot find the correct preposition. Yet he chooses to write in that language precisely because he believes in the coming together in the church of many cultures, and Greek is an instrument to that end.

In this respect, there is a difference between John and Paul. Both stand at the border between cultures; but Paul is more like today's mestizo, and John is more like today's immigrant. Paul is more at home than John in the Greek language and culture. He is a Roman citizen and also a citizen of Tarsus. Each of those citizenships entails certain privileges. John, on the other hand, probably grew up in Judea. We do not know how long he had lived in Asia when he wrote his book. The process of his mestizaje is at an earlier stage than that of Paul. Today, in some immigrant communities in the United States, people speak of the first, the second, and the 1.5 generations. John seems to belong to the first generation.

Perhaps that helps explain John's harsher attitude toward the culture and society around him. Immigrants from other cultures are often quite grateful for the welcome they have received; but no matter how well they are received or how grateful they are, they often are privileged with a critical perspective that allows them to see the darker side of the host culture—which is one reason why natives often resent them. As we shall see in another chapter, John was able to perceive in the surrounding society dimensions that others did not perceive. Although the traditional interpretation of the book of Revelation is that it was written in a situation of persecution, more recent scholarship tends to think that, though there were difficulties, it is John who is stressing the contrast between the church and the surrounding society to the point that persecution would become almost inevitable. This more recent interpretation has to do with a reevaluation of the reign of Domitian. Traditionally Domitian, during whose reign John most likely wrote his book, has been depicted as a tyrant with dreams of grandeur who among many other cruelties and depredations persecuted the church. Today scholars point out that practically all the non-

Christian literature describing Domitian as a tyrant is the product of a later dynasty trying to justify itself, and therefore is not very reliable. As to what Christian literature asserts, there does seem to have been some persecution under Domitian, but not as widespread as was previously believed. Thus, while Christians in Asia probably faced many difficulties, and perhaps even a measure of persecution, that was not the general state of the church when John wrote his book. On the contrary, apparently John's worry was not so much that the church would be persecuted as that Christians might capitulate and become accommodated to society in order to avoid persecution.

Certainly, John has little hope that true believers will be able to function in the mainstream of society. In Revelation 13, he speaks of two beasts. The first is the beast from the sea, which as we have seen is probably a reference to Rome and her power. The second is the beast from the land, which "exercises all the authority of the first beast on its behalf, and it makes the earth and its inhabitants worship the first beast" (Rev 13:12). Thus, this second beast represents the actual authority of Rome as it was exercised in Asia Minor by local authorities. This beast "causes all, both small and great, both rich and poor, both free and slave, to be marked on the right hand or the forehead, so that no one can buy or sell who does not have the mark" (Rev 13:16-17). In other words, in order to participate in the economic life of society at large one has to bear the mark of the beast; and, conversely, those who refuse to bear that mark, the faithful believers, will be excluded from that life.

As a Judean immigrant, John must have been shocked at the cultural accommodations of otherwise supposedly faithful Jews as well as Christians of Gentile origin. He

would see points of conflict that others could not see. To the
church in Smyrna he speaks of the "slander on the part of
those who say that they are Jews and are not, but are a synagogue of Satan" (Rev 2:9). Philadelphia also receives a message about "those of the synagogue of Satan who say they
are Jews and are not, but are lying" (Rev 3:9). This has been
traditionally interpreted as an anti-Jewish statement, claiming that Christians are the true Jews, and all other Jews really belong to Satan. However, in view of John's own inclina-
tions, it would seem to refer most likely to Jews who from
his perspective appeared to have capitulated before the demands of the surrounding society. To Thyatira he writes
words of condemnation because that church tolerated "that
woman Jezebel, who calls herself a prophet and is teaching
and beguiling my servants to practice fornication [most likely idolatry] and to eat food sacrificed to idols" (Rev 2:20). In
all of this, John is calling the church in this alien land—alien
because it is not the heavenly city, and alien also because it
is not Judea—to be firm against the encroachments of the
surrounding society and values.

His book also shows that John was a prophet and a poet.
In ancient Israel, the two often went together. Although
there is little actual poetry in Revelation, its tone throughout is so poetic that, after Psalms, this is the book of the
Bible that has inspired most hymns. John's imagery is that of
a poet, even though unfortunately it has often been understood in terms of prosaic descriptions.

John, however, is also a prophet. What he writes he calls
"the words of the prophecy of this book" (Rev 22:18). This
does not mean, as many have understood, that he is spelling
out a timetable or a program for future events. John is a
prophet in the strict biblical sense: he speaks the words of

God to the people of God. In this speaking the word of God there certainly is much that refers to the endtime, but its purpose is to call to obedience the church of John's time. The book is prophetic in the sense that it purports to be a word from God given through Jesus Christ: "The revelation of Jesus Christ, which God gave him..." (Rev 1:1). The purpose of this revelation is "to show his servants what must soon take place"—in other words, not necessarily nor primarily what will take place at the end of time, but what John's readers themselves will have to face. As a prophet, John receives his vision "in the spirit," and "on the Lord's day" (Rev 1:10), which is precisely the day that he would normally have been in the midst of the congregation, fulfilling his public role as a prophet or preacher.

His word as a prophet is both a warning and a promise. It is a warning in that it alerts its readers to the dangers inherent in living in Asia Minor, in the midst of the Roman Empire. These dangers have to do mostly with the allure of the empire and of its attending powers. It is difficult for us to see the allure, because we tend to think of the beasts that John describes as hideous, and therefore hardly tempting. This is because we take those descriptions literally, when they are intended symbolically. A woman with ruby lips, pearl teeth, and emerald eyes would not be very attractive; however, in our cultural conventions all of these images are metaphors which every one of us understands and accepts. Likewise, when John describes "a beast rising out of the sea, having ten horns and seven heads; and on its horns were ten diadems, and on its heads were blasphemous names" (Rev 13:1), he is not depicting an obviously repulsive creature, but just the contrary. The horns, heads, and diadems are all positive symbols of power. The numbers seven and ten are both positive numbers, indicating plenitude. The point of the entire description is that although this beast (which, again, represents Roman might) may appear attractive, in fact it carries with it "blasphemous names." That the many heads and horns are not intended to be negative is shown by the fact that the Lamb is also described as "having seven horns and seven eyes" (Rev 5:6). The enticing character of evil, which appears clothed in good, becomes clear in the description of the beast from the land, which "had two horns like a lamb and spoke like a dragon" (Rev 13:11). In short, then, the warning is that although the surrounding society and culture, and the power structure that supports them, may appear quite attractive, they in fact are instruments of evil, and those who find it possible to participate fully in them bear the mark of the beast (Rev 13:16-17).

The promise is that, paradoxically, "the Lamb that was slaughtered" will be revealed to be in truth "the Lion of the tribe of Judah," who will overcome all the powers of evil, and bring to himself and to his banquet those who have been faithful to the end. It is on the basis of this promise that the entire book of Revelation seeks to instill both endurance and hope in its hearers and eventual readers. This promise is the main theme of the book. Since the promise is eschatological, the book certainly is eschatological; but that is not to say that it is a sort of program of events for the endtime.

Another aspect of the promise is the assurance that heaven is aware of the suffering of its faithful children. John is speaking of very specific conditions on earth: the abuse of power on the part of Rome and its representatives, the economic oppression that has raised the price of wheat to levels that the poor cannot afford, the divisions within the church. Of all of this, he tells his readers, God is aware. Notice that

the message to each of the seven churches in chapters 2 and
3 begins with the words of Jesus: "I know..." In the rest of
the book, we are told repeatedly that there is a connection
between heaven and earth, signified above all by the fact
that the Lamb who was slain on earth now rules in heaven,
and also by the prayers of the saints ascending to the altar of
God (Rev 5:8; 8:3-4).

John is also a worshiping member of his community of
faith. His vision takes place "on the Lord's day" (Rev 1:10),
when he normally would have been worshiping in the midst
of the congregation. Toward the end of this essay we shall
return to the significance of worship in Revelation. At this
point, let it suffice to mention that much of what John describes is the worship that takes place in heaven, and that
therefore his book has many liturgical references. Since the
worship of the church is intended to be a reflection and a
rehearsal of worship in heaven, it is possible to see numerous connections between Revelation and what we know of
early Christian worship. Indeed, it has been argued that
"the outline or plan according to which the visions unfold is
possibly...laid out in a scheme that follows the order of the
Church's Paschal liturgy."[9] Whether one accepts such a
claim or not, it is clear that Revelation includes much liturgical material. This is one of the reasons why it has inspired
so many liturgical and other hymns. Again, as with the case
of his allusions to Hebrew Scripture and tradition, it is possible that John is simply using language and images that are
so deeply ingrained within himself that they come out unbidden, thus giving to his entire book a liturgical flavor.

---

[9]Massey H. Shepherd, Jr., *The Paschal Liturgy and the Apocalypse*
(Richmond: John Knox Press, 1960), 77.

Finally, a word must be said about John's creativity. Scholars often speak of an entire literary genre which they call "apocalyptic," and which includes the Revelation of John as well as a number of other books of Jewish, Christian, and even sometimes Persian or other origin. It is true that there are many commonalities between John's Apocalypse and these various books taken as a whole. Significantly, however, even though the term "apocalyptic" is taken from the very first word of the Apocalypse of John, scholars also point out that his book is not strictly "apocalyptic" in the same sense as the others. At the very beginning, its genre is more epistolary, containing what purport to be seven letters to seven churches; yet there is no indication that these letters ever existed separately from the rest of the book, nor that they were intended solely for the church to which each was addressed. Furthermore, there are elements in Revelation that bring it closer to the classical prophets than to later apocalyptic literature. Therefore, if we are to give John of Patmos his due, we must say that, just as the author of the first gospel created a new literary genre, a different way of telling a story, so too did the author of Revelation, creating his own work out of many different strands, eventually producing a book that is in a class by itself—thus providing one more instance of a common phenomenon in the history of Christianity, namely, that some of the most creative theology develops at the edge, where mission occurs, where cultures meet, where mestizaje also develops.

V

Out of Every Tribe and Nation

John of Patmos may have been a Jew, writing to mostly Jewish churches; yet it is significant that no other book in the New Testament deals with the issue of the coming together of a variety of peoples and cultures as repeatedly nor as specifically as does the book of Revelation. Paradoxically, there is a connection between the two. It is precisely because he is deeply rooted in his culture and tradition that John has to come to grips with the multicultural challenge that he faces. If he did not care for his own culture and tradition, he might convince himself that cultures after all make no difference, that their variety is not important, that they can simply be ignored or assimilated. In a way, it is precisely because he is a Jew, and conscious of his own culture, that John has to come to grips with the variety of people included in this new people that God is creating. It is for this reason that we find *seven* times in his book, with slight variations, the theme of "every tribe and language and people and nation." And, because the issue is so pervasive, we do not find that listing always in similar contexts—not even always in positive contexts.

Before dealing specifically with that phrase, however, it is important to acknowledge the literary source of such a listing. Clearly, John the Seer has taken it from the book of Daniel, where a similar list appears several times. Indeed, one could summarize the argument of the first half of the book of Daniel by simply outlining the use of that "multi-cultural" phrase. It appears first in Daniel 3:4, where King Nebuchadnezzar orders that "peoples, nations, and languages" should fall down before the golden statue that he has set up and worship it. It appears again a few verses later, where we are told that in fact, "all the peoples, nations, and languages fell down and worshiped the golden statue that King Nebuchadnezzar had set up." At the beginning of chapter 4, after the king has been moved by the episode of the fiery furnace, he sends a message "to all peoples, nations, and languages" regarding the mighty acts of God. In chapter 5, the king is Belshazzar, and Daniel begins his explanation of the writing on the wall by declaring to the king that it was God who gave Nebuchadnezzar "kingship, greatness, glory, and majesty. And because of the greatness that he gave him, all peoples, nations, and languages trembled and feared before him." Finally, in chapter 6, King Darius writes "to all peoples and nations of every language throughout the world," ordering "that in all my royal dominion people should tremble and fear before the God of Daniel."

Thus the plot of this section in the book of Daniel could be summarized as a struggle regarding who has real authority over the peoples, nations, and languages. At the outset, the king orders them to worship an idol, and they obey. But then the same king comes to understand that God is more powerful than the king himself, and issues a decree to all peoples, nations, and languages letting them know that it is so. Then, in the next generation, another king refuses to acknowledge that it was God who gave his father power over all peoples, nations, and languages, and he therefore loses his kingdom. Finally, his successor acknowledges what Nebuchadnezzar learned only through the episode of the fiery furnace, and what Belshazzar refused to learn.

There is a parallel between this plot and the book of Revelation. Just as in Daniel Nebuchadnezzar claims authority over all peoples and nations, and these seem to agree by worshiping the statue that the king has raised, so does the beast claim similar authority in Revelation; and, as we shall see, the tribes, peoples, languages, and nations do worship the beast. And, just as in Daniel King Darius in the end writes to all the various peoples and nations of every language that they "should tremble and fear before the God of Daniel," so in John's Revelation the final vision is one in which all peoples, tribes, and nations worship the One who sits on the throne.

Therefore, a study of the phrase "every nation and tribe and language and people" and its variants in the book of Revelation may help us understand much of the message of that book.

Let us begin with Revelation 14:6-7:

Then I saw another angel flying in midheaven, with an eternal gospel to proclaim to those who live on the earth—to every nation and tribe and language and people. He said in a loud voice, "Fear God and give him glory, for the hour of his judgment has come; and worship him who made heaven and earth, the sea and the springs of water."

This must have been a rather surprising vision for John. Since we do not know beyond any doubt exactly who John of Patmos was, he may or may not have been among the eleven who went to meet Jesus on a mountain in Galilee, there to receive the Great Commission: "Go therefore and make disciples of all nations." But, whether he was John the Apostle or another John, he must have known of that Great Commission which Jesus gave, not only to those first eleven, but also through them to the entire church. Whether directly or through others, he had received from Jesus the commission to preach the gospel to all the nations, making disciples and baptizing them.

But now it turns out that the mission of proclaiming the gospel throughout the world does not belong to the disciples alone, nor even to the entire church. In the last days it has been entrusted to an angel flying in midheaven, with an eternal gospel to proclaim to those who live on the earth—to every nation and tribe and language and people.

The visionary on Patmos to whom the proclamation of the gospel has been entrusted, the leader of the church commissioned to continue the task of that proclamation, now learns that the work of proclaiming the gospel is not to be carried out by humans alone, but also by an angel flying in midheaven.

If John thought of himself as an evangelist, the same way many of us today think of ourselves as evangelists, he might have been dismayed. We convince ourselves that, if we can somehow preach the gospel with more fervor, with more eloquence, with more conviction, people will necessarily listen. Some even go on television arguing that all that is needed is more money for better communication technologies, for more powerful transmitters, for more stations to carry their programs. Some professors of evangelism impress on us the importance of proper techniques as part of responsible evangelism. And that may all be partially true. But, lest we take it too seriously, lest we take ourselves too seriously, it is helpful to remember that here we have no less an evangelist than an angel, an angel flying in midheaven, proclaiming the gospel "to every nation and tribe and language and people." This angel is proclaiming the gospel with the support of all sorts of portents that have come to confirm it. And even after this angel finishes his task, with far more resources than the most powerful television station, even then, there are still enough who refuse to believe to keep the seven angels with the seven plagues busy! In a way, this is a passage to cut every professional evangelist and even every would-be apostle down to size.

The text holds still another surprise. It speaks of an angel with an eternal gospel—that is, an angel with tremendous, unequalled good news. And what does this good news angel say? He says: "Fear God!" The very first word of the angel's good news is fear!

This seems to contradict the very idea of good news! It certainly moves in the opposite direction from the angel who said to the shepherds guarding their flocks at night: "Fear not, for I bring you news of great joy." The Christmas angel brings good news that will cast out fear. The angel in Revelation brings good news that begins with fear: "Fear God and give him glory, for the hour of his judgment has come." Fear makes sense in this connection, for the angel is announcing God's judgment. And yet, this announcement is "an eternal gospel," good news!

This good-news/bad-news story is to be proclaimed "to those who live on earth—to every nation and tribe and language and people." In some ways, this combines the elements of pluralism that we see in the Great Commission with those we see in Pentecost. The gospel is to be proclaimed to nations, as in Matthew, and to languages, as in Acts. And this is not just a missionary strategy, as some have interpreted Paul in 1 Corinthians. It is not a strategy for church growth. It is not the church's response to growing pluralism in society. It is the very purpose of God, carried forth by an angel in midheaven.

There are, however, other passages which are not so positive in their evaluation of the many tribes, nations, peoples, and languages. It is important to recall these, for otherwise we are in danger of romanticizing cultures and multiculturalism, and forgetting that they too have their demonic dimensions.

In Revelation 11, John offers the vision of the two witnesses. It is not necessary for our purposes here to enter into the discussion as to what or whom these two witnesses might represent. What is important is that, after the two witnesses have completed their testimony and been killed, "for three and a half days members of the peoples and tribes and languages and nations will gaze at their dead bodies and refuse to let them be placed in a tomb; and the inhabitants of the earth will gloat over them and exchange presents, because these two prophets had been a torment to the inhabitants of the earth." In other words, if the glory of heaven is to be shared by a great multitude out of every tribe and nation and people and language, so too the Lamb and its witnesses are to be opposed by others out of every people and tribe and language and nation. (In passing, it may be well to remember that also in the book of Daniel "all the peoples, nations, and languages fell down and worshiped the golden statue that King Nebuchadnezzar had set up" [Dn 3:7].) Multiculturalism may be an important trait of the very nature of the church, but it is also an important trait of the powers of evil.

Revelation 13 makes that point even clearer. There John is speaking of the beast from the sea. As suggested above, this otherwise enigmatic "beast from the sea" is not so mysterious when one takes into account that, from the point of view of Asia Minor, Roman power and Roman commands came from the sea. At any rate, this beast appears to be all-powerful, and is therefore worshiped by the whole earth. Accordingly, John says: "It [that is, the beast] was given authority over every tribe and people and language and nation, and all the inhabitants of the earth will worship it, everyone whose name has not been written from the foundation of the world in the book of life of the Lamb that was slaughtered." (And, again, note the parallel between John's wording, to the effect that the beast "was given" such "authority over every tribe and people and language and nation," and Daniel's assertion that it was God who gave Nebuchadnezzar such greatness that "all peoples, nations, and languages trembled and feared before him" [Dn 5:19].)

The glorious multitude dressed in white robes and singing hymns to the Lamb represents every tribe and people and language and nation. But so does the multitude that bows before the beast and adores it.

Next, let us look at Revelation 17. This is the vision of the great harlot. As in every such vision, the details are confusing, and not always consistent with each other. For instance, the harlot is sitting on a red beast, and that is the way she is usually depicted. But the angel also tells John that she is "the great whore who is seated on many waters."

This is obviously an allusion to Jeremiah 51:13, where the prophet is speaking against Babylon: "You who live by mighty waters, rich in treasures, your end has come." It is also a reference to a theme that appears repeatedly in ancient iconography, where a city is often depicted as a goddess enthroned by a river.[1] The reason for this is that in ancient times most long distance transportation took place by water rather than by land. We read much about the famous Roman roads, whose remains can be seen to this day in rugged mountain passes all over Western Europe. But economically those famous roads were not half as important as the waterways. Roads were intended for moving armies and their supplies, and also sometimes for connecting areas where water transport was difficult or impossible. In the East, caravans carrying luxury items from the Orient traveled by land. But by far the vast majority of trade in the Roman Empire took place through water transport. Indeed, it was far more expensive to carry a heavy load by oxcart for a hundred miles along a mountain road than to transport it by ship from one end of the empire to the other. This is the reason why Chrysostom praises God for having created "the shorter route of the sea."[2] It is also why at a very early date Rome began shipping wheat from faraway Sicily and then from Egypt, rather than carting it from the much closer fertile valleys of the Apennines. This led Columella to complain, much as North Americans complain today about Japanese imports: "In this Latium, land of Saturn, where the gods taught their own descendants the art of agricul-

---

[1]Ford, *Revelation*, 277. Ford, however, argues that the harlot represents Jerusalem rather than Rome—a view that has not convinced many.

[2]*Ad Dem.*, 2.5.

ture, we now must hold auctions for the carting of wheat from provinces beyond the sea."[3]

Water is also a symbol of chaos. In many Near Eastern myths of creation, the gods begin by conquering the chaos of the waters. In Genesis, one of God's first acts in ordering creation is to separate the waters and set limits to them. The image of a city sitting on many waters would then indicate that such a city keeps down the threat of chaos—a chaos that would arise were the many peoples, tribes, and nations allowed free rein to go their own ways. In other words, it is a reference to the much vaunted *pax Romana*.

Thus, to depict the great harlot as "seated on many waters" was another way of saying that it was a rich city, a city to which, as in ancient Babylon, all the riches of the world flowed. And it was also another way of saying that this could be justified on the basis of the order and security it produced.

There follows the familiar description of the great harlot, and then the angel explains the meaning of the vision to John. The ten horns, for instance, are petty rulers, kinglets whom the great harlot appoints, and who enjoy their power from her, but who will eventually turn against her. And, says the angel, "The waters that you saw, where the whore is seated, are peoples and multitudes and nations and languages" (Rev 17:15). In other words, the great harlot is rich, but she is rich because she sits on all these various nations and cultures, exploiting them and having their wealth flow to her like many waters.

What do we learn from all of this about what it means to be a multicultural church in a multicultural society? We cer-

---

[3]*De re rust.* 1, *praef.*

tainly learn that we must not romanticize culture and multi-culturalism.

There are at least three ways in which we are often inclined to such romanticization.

The first is by claiming for cultures—for our culture, or for any other culture—a purity which cultures by nature do not have. Cultures and languages and nations and peoples are historical phenomena. They are part of this fallen creation. And, as part of fallen creation, they carry in their very being the sign of sin.

I love my culture. Yet, when I stop to think about it, I realize that my culture, and the Spanish language of which I am so proud and which I so love, are in many ways the result and the distillation of many an oppression. If I speak Spanish, it is because my Spanish ancestors invaded the lands of my Indian ancestors, suppressing their language and traditions, and trying to erase their culture, as if it had never existed. And, if the Spanish I speak still includes some native words that would have sounded strange to sixteenth-century Spanish conquistadors, it is because, even after five hundred years, the culture of my Indian ancestors has refused to let itself be entirely obliterated. But I can go further back. The reason why I call my hand *mano* is because, even before the advent of the church, my Roman ancestors conquered my Celtiberian ancestors. And the reason why I call cheese *queso,* and not something like *fromaggio,* is that my Visigothic ancestors conquered my Roman ancestors. And the reason why, when I wish to say "may God will it," I say *ojalá,* even from a Christian pulpit, is that my Moorish ancestors conquered my Visigothic ancestors.

I love my culture. I love my language. I am enthralled by the richness and the fluidity with which it can express the most varied tones and moods. But I must remember: this language and this culture which I so love are the result of much pain and many an oppression.

It is important for us to remember this, for otherwise love of language and culture runs the risk of becoming demonic. It is when we forget this that love of language and culture results in ethnic cleansing, in theories of supremacy, and in racial and cultural exclusivism. It is important to remember this, for language and culture properly understood are to be represented in the great throng singing the praises of the Lamb; but language and culture turned into objects of idolatry are among the most insidious tools of the beast and the dragon.

Second, we tend to romanticize cultures by claiming for them a stability which they do not have. Culture is by definition a living thing, and a living thing is always changing. Cultures are by nature permeable, just as skin is permeable. They influence each other. They evolve as the world and society evolve. A culture that cannot evolve is dead, and is no longer a real culture, but the relic of a culture. This is perhaps the greatest problem that I encounter as I deal with people of my own cultural tradition who have come to this country, and who now feel the pain of watching their children be influenced by things which the parents do not understand. "They are losing their culture," they tell me. To which probably the only answer is: "Perhaps they are creating a culture. Perhaps it will be through this encounter that the culture of their ancestors will find new expression." Certainly, if a culture is only a relic of times past and of circumstances which no longer exist, it is no longer a living culture.

Finally, there is a third way in which we tend to romanticize culture. That is by forgetting that culture always exists in a political and economic context. John of Patmos seems to be well aware of this: "The waters where the whore is seated are peoples and multitudes and nations and languages."

If we accept the most common interpretation, that the great harlot is the city of Rome and its imperial power, it follows that John of Patmos has a very realistic understanding of the wealth of Rome. Rome is wealthy, not because she is particularly productive, and certainly not because her people work harder than the many peoples, tribes, nations, and languages she has subjected, but rather because she has devised a system whereby the wealth of all these nations flows to Rome, as so many rivers.

As was shown in chapter 2, the first century was a time of great mixing of cultures. Nowhere was this mixture more evident than in Rome itself, where people from all over the empire converged. We also know that the more aristocratic and traditional Romans bemoaned the fact that their city was being overrun by all these people of various tribes, and nations, and languages. At approximately the same time when John was at Patmos, or shortly thereafter, Tacitus complained—as already noted—that Rome was a cesspool to which flowed everything that was sordid and degrading from every corner of the earth. Others took the opposite tack, accepting quite wholeheartedly at least some of the elements of foreign culture that were invading even the most traditional quarters of Rome. But it was John of Patmos who most clearly saw that the nations and tribes and peoples and languages were present in Rome, not simply for cultural exchange, but also because Rome was the great harlot sitting on many waters, and the many waters were the "peoples and multitudes and nations and languages" who actually produced the wealth that made the harlot great.

John of Patmos was well aware of the economic hardships which the Roman Empire caused for the poor. Rome considered itself the great civilizer, which is to say, the great "cityfier," for as the Romans saw it the city was the greatest invention of antiquity. Yet for cities to be built, the countryside had to pay. While wages remained fairly constant, taxes and inflation took an increasing toll on the rural poor. In Egypt, for instance, where a peasant's lot had never been easy, things became much worse under Roman rule. The time soon came when the normal wage for a rural worker, 2 oboli a day, could buy only seven-tenths of a liter of unhulled wheat—enough to make a small loaf of bread—and out of that amount the rural worker had to pay taxes of at least 135 oboli a year—roughly the equivalent of 67 days of work. In other provinces the situation was no better.

The book of Revelation records a protest in Asia Minor against such conditions. In Revelation 6:5-6 we read:

When he opened the third seal, I heard the third living creature call out, "Come!" I looked, and there was a black horse! Its rider held a pair of scales in his hand, and I heard what seemed to be a voice in the midst of the four living creatures saying, "A quart of wheat for a day's pay, and three quarts of barley for a day's pay, but do not damage the olive oil and the wine!"

To understand this passage, it helps to remember that when the King of Pergamum bequeathed most of Asia Minor to the Roman Republic, the region was rich and prosperous. Its main exports were wools and dyestuffs, and its fertile lands grew sufficient wheat for all its population.

Yet, as the region became integrated with the rest of the empire, rich landlords realized that acreage devoted to grapes and olives resulted in much greater income than the same acreage planted with grain. Slowly, but inexorably, the land moved into the hands of a few rich owners who devoted more and more of it to grapevines and olive trees. Grain became scarce and the province, though rich because of its exports of wine and olive oil, was poor in that there was not enough to eat. In the year 92 C.E., Emperor Domitian issued a decree ordering that half the vineyards in the provinces be destroyed, precisely with the purpose of promoting grain production. But the landed aristocracy raised such an outcry that the emperor rescinded his decree.[4] The result was even greater scarcity of grain and greater misery for the poor. The normal price of wheat was twelve quarts for a denarius; and barley, which was used mostly for animal feed and for humans only in times of economic difficulty, was supposed to be twenty-four quarts for a denarius. Thus, what the "living creature" says in Revelation 6:6 is a strong protest against an inflationary process that has made the price of wheat rise by 1200 percent, and the price of barley rise by 800 percent: "A quart of wheat for a day's pay, and three quarts of barley for a day's pay, but do not damage the olive oil and the wine!" Furthermore, the rider against whom the living creature raises such a challenge carries in his hands, not a bow like the first rider nor a sword like the second, but a pair of scales, symbol of the trade that has made the landed aristocracy rich and the poor classes even poorer, bringing a devasta-

---

[4]Suetonius, *Dom.* 7.2; Statius, *Silv.* 4.3.11-12; Eusebius, *Chron.* 2.160.

tion comparable to war and to that wrought by the riders of the first two horses, warriors who carry a bow and a sword. The cultural encounters of the first century, and those of our day, do not take place in abstraction of economic and political systems. It is not just that world travel has become easier, and therefore people of different cultures meet more often than they used to. It is also that the world order—or rather, the world disorder—is such that people are forced to leave their traditional homes and move to new lands in search of safety, security, freedom, and work. All other things being equal, most people would rather live where they grew up, in their own homelands and in the context of their own cultures. But all things are not equal, and therefore people cross borders and even oceans seeking the safety and the opportunities that are often denied them in their own homelands. When the rivers of wealth flow in one direction, it is only natural for population to flow in the same direction.

Examples abound. In the last twenty years, thousands and thousands of acres in Mexico that were once used for growing corn and beans and other such staples for local consumption are now used to grow vegetables and flowers for export to the United States. As vegetables flow from Mexico across the border, growers north of the border find it difficult to compete, and must seek cheaper labor. That labor is then provided by Mexican workers, probably the same workers who until recently were growing beans in Mexico, but have now been displaced by the mechanized production of export crops and are looking for work. Thus, while the newspapers carry all sorts of reports about people crossing illegally under the bridge, those people are in a sense following the tomatoes that are crossing legally over the bridge. Where the rivers of wealth flow, there too flow the rivers of population.

Something similar is happening in Great Britain and France, where there is now a strong backlash against all the immigrants who are coming to those countries from their former colonies. The Europeans may not like it; but the reason why such migrations are taking place, and precisely to those particular countries, is that those very countries previously colonized the lands from which the immigrants are coming. For decades, the colonial powers were enriched with the wealth of the world. Today, they should not be surprised by the resulting demographical shifts. Where the rivers of wealth flow, there too flow the rivers of population.

John of Patmos had it right. The multicultural society of the Roman Empire was not just the result of cultural exchange. It was also the result of economic exchange supported by military might. And, in some ways, the same is true of the multicultural society of the twentieth century. It is the result of European conquest and westward expansion. It is the result of black slavery and the trade that supported it. It is the result of colonialism in the nineteenth century, and of economic neocolonialism in the twentieth. It is the result of two world wars and a cold one. It is the result of civil wars in Central America, fostered by the great superpowers. Thus, when we look at our present-day communities and see them as multicultural, multiethnic microcosms in which all the nations, cultures, languages, and people of the world meet, it is important to realize that these communities are also the result of the vast forces, mostly evil forces, that have uprooted people and tossed them upon distant shores. A multiethnic society is a microcosm, not only of ethnic diversity throughout the world, but also of the strife, injustice, and oppression that rule the world—or as John of Patmos would say, of the power of the beast.

Yet it is not only with economic issues that John has to deal as he faces the multicultural challenge. He also has to deal with his own culture and tradition. In Revelation 10 we read:

And I saw another mighty angel coming down from heaven, wrapped in a cloud, with a rainbow over his head; his face was like the sun, and his legs like pillars of fire. [2]He held a little scroll open in his hand. Setting his right foot on the sea and his left foot on the land, [3]he gave a great shout, like a lion roaring. And when he shouted, the seven thunders sounded. [4]And when the seven thunders had sounded, I was about to write, but I heard a voice from heaven saying, "Seal up what the seven thunders have said, and do not write it down." [5]Then the angel whom I saw standing on the sea and the land raised his right hand to heaven [6]and swore by him who lives forever and ever, who created heaven and what is in it, the earth and what is in it, and the sea and what is in it: "There will be no more delay, [7]but in the days when the seventh angel is to blow his trumpet, the mystery of God will be fulfilled, as he announced to his servants the prophets." [8]Then the voice that I had heard from heaven spoke to me again, saying, "Go, take the scroll that is open in the hand of the angel who is standing on the sea and on the land." [9]So I went to the angel and told him to give me the little scroll; and he said to me, "Take it, and eat; it will be bitter to your stomach, but sweet as honey in your mouth." [10]So I took the little scroll from the hand of the angel and ate it; it was sweet as honey in my mouth, but when I had eaten it, my stomach was made bitter. [11]Then they said to me, "You must prophesy again about many peoples and nations and languages and kings."

Clearly, this passage is patterned after Ezekiel 2 and 3, where the prophet is given a scroll to eat. But before we turn to that text, we must look at John's vision of the little scroll in the context of the book of Revelation itself.

This is a "little scroll." And it is open. It is not the great scroll with the seven seals, which only the victorious Lamb can open. Furthermore, it is held in the hand of an angel. It is not like the great scroll with the seven seals, which is held by the right hand of the One who sits on the throne and passed directly from the Almighty God to the Almighty Lamb. Presumably, this little scroll does not contain the entire mystery of history, as the larger scroll does. It is much more modest than that. It is the word given to John to proclaim to the churches. In order to proclaim God's message to the churches, John does not need to digest the entire scroll with the seven seals. Indeed, in this very vision of the little scroll there is an episode in which "the seven thunders" sound with a mighty voice, and John prepares to write what he has heard. But he is told not to write. Scholars debate what that may mean. But whatever it means, it clearly implies that what John is to proclaim is much humbler than any such grandiose vision. What he is to proclaim is the word which he has digested and assimilated in this little scroll.

Here again the role of the prophet/evangelist is put in its proper context. It is a very important role—so important that a mighty angel brings it. But the prophet does not get to eat the great scroll with the seven seals. And, as we saw in another passage, he is not the only one proclaiming the eternal gospel.

If we now compare this passage with its literary background in Ezekiel 2 and 3, the parallels are obvious. There is no need to dwell on them. What is more striking, however, are two significant differences. The first is that, while Ezekiel says "I ate it, and in my mouth it was as sweet as honey," John says: "It was sweet as honey in my mouth, but when I had eaten it, my stomach was made bitter." Ezekiel speaks of a sweet word of God. For John, the word he is to proclaim is bittersweet.

The second difference has to do with the scope of the message of each of the two prophets. Ezekiel is told: "Mortal, go to the house of Israel and speak my very words to them. For you are not sent to a people of obscure speech and difficult language, but to the house of Israel—not to many peoples of obscure speech and difficult language, whose words you cannot understand." In contrast, the mighty angel tells John: "You must prophesy again about many peoples and nations and languages and kings."

There are a number of theories as to why John says that the scroll made his stomach bitter. One possibility is that the word he receives is a word of judgment. Although it is sweet because it is the word of God, it is bitter because it is a word of destruction and death. This is an attractive theory, although the truth is that Ezekiel's word is equally of judgment, for he says that in the scroll which he ate were written "words of lamentation and mourning and woe." Thus, if John's scroll was bitter for that reason, Ezekiel's should have been too. Another theory is that the scroll is bitter in John's stomach because it contains words about the persecution and suffering that Christians are to undergo. That too is an attractive theory.

I prefer, however, to see a connection between the two particular traits in John's vision vis-à-vis Ezekiel's: the bitterness in the stomach and the wide scope of the message. If any writer of the New Testament was a Jew, and steeped in Jewish culture and traditions, that was John of Patmos. It has been pointed out that there is hardly a verse in his book that does not have an allusion to the Hebrew Scriptures. His Greek is full of Hebraisms, perhaps due in part to his greater familiarity with Hebrew and with Aramaic, and perhaps as a result of his constant literary dependence on the Hebrew Bible. And he quotes that Bible, not from the Septuagint that all the other New Testament authors employed, but either from an unknown translation or from his own, which he does as he goes along.

He is well aware of the mission given to the prophet Ezekiel when he ate his scroll: Ezekiel was to speak only to the house of Israel, and they would not believe him. Now he, John, is not told to whom he is to speak, but about whom. As one looks at the Greek text, one notes that John uses the preposition *epi*. With that preposition, a genitive case would have meant that John was to prophesy *to* many peoples and nations and languages and kings. An accusative case would have meant that he was to prophesy *against* them. But the dative case, used here, means that he is to prophesy *about* them, as the NRSV correctly translates.[5]

---

[5]Professor Eugene Boring, of Texas Christian University's Brite Divinity School, has provided me with significant insight regarding John's use of the preposition *epi* in this particular passage, as well as in others. His

The difference between Ezekiel's vision and John's is not that Ezekiel is to go to Israel, to a people who understand his language, and John is to go throughout the world, to many peoples and nations and languages and kings. The difference is rather that John is to go back to his audience, presumably the seven churches and other similar communities in Asia, and speak to them *about* the many peoples and nations and languages and kings. This may be understood in the sense in which Amos preaches about the various surrounding peoples: the message is certainly not always positive; but the very fact that God deals with these other people places Israel in a different light. And that is why the word of God, the little scroll that will be John's message, although sweet to the taste, is hard to stomach.

John the Jew, John who can effortlessly quote the Hebrew Scriptures backward and forward, is given a message to proclaim to his congregations. His congregations are probably also mostly Jewish. Otherwise, they would hardly be able to understand this book he is writing to them, so full of allusions to the Hebrew Scriptures, and even to more re-

---

conclusion is that the translation "about" is correct, although this is to be understood in the sense of "directed toward," and not in the sense of "providing information about." It is probably John's rendering of the Old Testament phrase "prophesy against." This does not mean, however, that John is to go to these nations and speak to them, just as Amos does not go to the various nations and speak to them. Nor does it necessarily mean that the message is purely negative. It means, rather, that these various nations are confronted by God, just as Israel is confronted by God. At any rate, no matter what the most accurate translation of this particular phrase might be, it is clear that John's entire book is speaking to his mostly Jewish congregations about the many tribes and nations, and not directly to the nations themselves.

cent Jewish traditions. And now he is told that he is to speak
to these congregations, not just the word they expect, that
those who are faithful until death will receive the crown of
life, or that everyone who conquers will receive some of the
hidden manna and a white stone with a secret name, but he
is to speak to them about "many peoples and nations and
languages and kings." He is to speak to them, not only about
how important it is that they be faithful in the impending
tribulations and persecution, but also about God's judgment
over all the peoples who worship the beast, a judgment that
is a sign of God's love for the many "saints from every tribe
and language and people and nation," whom the Lamb has
made "to be a kingdom and priests serving our God," and
who "will reign on earth" (Rev 5:9-10).

This is perhaps the most difficult aspect of becoming a
multicultural church in a multicultural world. Bringing people in from other nations and tribes and peoples and languages is not difficult, as long as they are brought into the
same church, dominated by the same nation and tribe and
people and language. Throughout its history, whenever the
church has taken the Great Commission seriously, it has
been willing and even eager to prophesy *to* many nations,
tribes, and peoples. It has also been willing to prophesy *in*
many languages, and to that end missionaries have translated the Bible into thousands of languages, and have even devised writing systems for hundreds of languages that had
none. We have certainly taken to heart the task of going
throughout the world and preaching the gospel to every
creature. To that task many of our great missionaries have
devoted their entire lives, and even sacrificed them. For
that task, we continually collect offerings in our churches.
And there are many in our congregations right now who

complain that we are not doing enough of it, and argue that we should try to recover our first love for missions. Be that as it may, in this passage that is not what John is told to do. He is *not* told to go and speak *to* many peoples, nations, languages, and kings. He is told, rather, to speak to his congregations *about* many peoples, nations, languages, and kings. And he finds that bitter to his stomach.

The difficult task facing us today, as we seek to be faithful in today's world, is *not*, as some might imagine, bringing ethnic minorities into the Christian community, nor is it even creating and sustaining ethnic minority ministries and parishes. Actually, it is quite presumptuous on the part of those in the dominant culture to assume that it is up to them to determine whether or not the gospel will make headway among other cultures and peoples. Not only is it presumptuous; it is also clearly wrongheaded. The fact is that the gospel *is* making headway among the many tribes, peoples, nations, and languages—that it is indeed making more headway among them than it is among the dominant cultures of the North Atlantic. The question is not whether there will be a multicultural church. Rather, the question is whether those who have become accustomed to seeing the gospel expressed only or primarily in terms of those dominant cultures will be able to participate in the life of the multicultural church that is already a reality.

For persons of the dominant culture, the most difficult part is—as it was also for John of Patmos—telling their own people about the many peoples and nations and languages who are also called to be part of the great multitude that worships the Lamb. And telling them in such a way that they realize that, no matter what they may have thought, their own people and tribe and nation and language is no

more in God's plan than *one* of the many peoples and tribes
and nations and languages whom God is calling to make, as
Revelation would say, "a kingdom of priests serving God."

It is easy to speak the word of a multicultural church in
a multicultural society in such a way that it is sweet as honey
in our mouth. And it should be. There is beauty, and joy,
and fullness, in many people coming together, out of every
tribe and nation and people and language. But if we remain
there, if somehow we avoid that part of the same word
which is bitter to the stomach, we are not faithful to John's
vision. The vision which John the Jew has is a vision of a
Gentile church, a church where the Gentiles, the nations, *ta
ethne*, the *goyim*, will come and take their place right next
to the tribes of Israel, and all together will claim the ancient
promise made to the people of Israel, that they would be a
kingdom of priests. That is a vision sweet as honey, for it
shows the fullness of the mercy of God; but it is also a vision
bitter to the stomach, because it shows that no people, no
tribe, no language, no nation, can claim a place of particular
honor in that fullness. And it is bittersweet, because it involves radical change in the very congregations where John
has served and which he loves.

And so it is with us today. The multicultural vision is
sweet. But there is also a bitter side to it. There is the bitter
side of having to declare that the vision of many peoples,
many tribes, many nations, and many languages involves
much more than bringing a bit of color and folklore into our
traditional worship services. It involves radical changes in
the way we understand ourselves, and in the way we run our
business.

There is, however, another factor that must be pointed
out. Although it is true that in a sense John's profound ap-

preciation for his Jewish background may make it difficult
for him to stomach the vision of many tribes, many peoples,
many nations, and many languages, it is also true, paradoxically enough, that he can be true to that vision only and precisely because he has that profound appreciation for his
own culture. The apostle Paul is free to be a Jew to the
Jews, and as one outside the Law to those outside the Law,
because he can claim to be "circumcised on the eighth day,
a member of the people of Israel, of the tribe of Benjamin,
a Hebrew born of Hebrews, as to the law, a Pharisee, ... as
to righteousness under the law, blameless" (Phil 3:5-6). If
we are to develop a truly multicultural church, each one of
us must begin by having a profound appreciation of her or
his own culture. It is very difficult to become multicultural
when one is not even cultural—when one is not deeply
rooted in the traditions and values that have sustained one's
people through generations, when one does not resonate to
the central symbols of one's culture.

This is something I have come to understand as I have
worked with people training to be missionaries among
Spanish-speaking people. When I meet a candidate who ap-
preciates her own language and culture, I know that she will
be able to catch a glimpse of the beauty of my language and
culture. But when I meet a candidate who has not even
taken the trouble to learn English properly, whose heart
does not throb at the subtleties of Shakespeare or the ca-
dences of Longfellow, I lose hope of ever being able to
make him understand how I feel about my own language,
about the rhythms that I heard in the cradle, or the sonnets
which Lope de Vega addressed to the Crucified.

John of Patmos, who apparently cannot speak without
quoting the ancient literature of his people, can understand

both the joy and the pain of a vision where "saints from every tribe and language and people and nation" have been made "a kingdom of priests serving God" (Rev 5:9-10). What we need today, if we are to become the truly multicultural church we are called to be even within the confines of the United States, is a Jane Smith of Delaware who is deeply rooted in her Anglo culture, who shares and claims both the glories and the horrors, the bittersweetness of her tradition. And we need her to work with John Smith of Columbus, who shares and claims the glories and the horrors, the bittersweetness of his African-American ancestry. And we need them to work with Juana Pérez of Cincinnati, and with John Silverfox of Cleveland, and with Jung Young Kim of Dayton, all of whom share and claim the glories and the horrors, the bittersweetness of their respective traditions. And together, and separately, we must each and all take the little scroll, that portion of God's message entrusted to us, and eat it, and digest it, and rejoice at the sweetness in our mouths, and wonder at the bitterness in our stomachs, for we, like John, are called to go and "prophesy again about many peoples and nations and languages and kings."

VI

Our Eyes Have Seen the Glory

We have been attempting a multicultural reading of the book of Revelation—or rather, a reading of our multicultural situation through the lens of the book of Revelation. We looked first of all at that strange text in Revelation 14 which declares that the preaching of the gospel "to every nation and tribe and language and people" is not just the task of the church and of its preachers, but is also the task of angels. Then we looked at three other very realistic texts that depict the situation as the seer in Patmos was living it, and also as we today are living it. These may be called the "negative" texts about every tribe and nation and language and people. They are the two texts from Revelation 11 and 13 which declare that all the tribes and nations worship the beast and reject the witnesses sent by God; and, perhaps most realistic of all, the passage in Revelation 17 which declares that the harlot sits on many waters, and that the waters on which she sits are the many tribes and peoples and nations and languages which must bring their treasures to her. In John's time, as throughout history and even in our day, much multicultural encounter has been the result of imperial expansion and colonial exploitation.

Then we looked at a slightly different passage, in which the prophet is told that his specific task is to go and speak "about many peoples and nations and languages and kings," and the taste of it is bitter to his stomach.

In all of these passages, John seems to be speaking of things as they were in his time, as they have been throughout history, and as they are to this day. Now we turn to two rather different passages in which the phrase that we have been following appears. They are different in that they are set in heaven, at the end of time, in the feast of the Lamb.

The first of these two passages is in Revelation 5:6-14:

Then I saw between the throne and the four living creatures and among the elders a Lamb standing as if it had been slaughtered, having seven horns and seven eyes, which are the seven spirits of God sent out into all the earth. [7]He went and took the scroll from the right hand of the one who was seated on the throne. [8]When he had taken the scroll, the four living creatures and the twenty-four elders fell before the Lamb, each holding a harp and golden bowls full of incense, which are the prayers of the saints. [9]They sing a new song: "You are worthy to take the scroll and to open its seals, for you were slaughtered and by your blood you ransomed for God saints from every tribe and language and people and nation; [10]you have made them to be a kingdom and priests serving our God, and they will reign on earth." [11]Then I looked, and I heard the voice of many angels surrounding the throne and

the living creatures and the elders; they numbered
myriads of myriads and thousands of thousands,
[12]singing with full voice, "Worthy is the Lamb that
was slaughtered to receive power and wealth and
wisdom and might and honor and glory and blessing!" [13]Then I heard every creature in heaven and
on earth and under the earth and in the sea, and all
that is in them, singing, "To the one seated on the
throne and to the Lamb be blessing and honor and
glory and might forever and ever!" [14]And the four
living creatures said, "Amen!" And the elders fell
down and worshiped.

The second passage appears in Revelation 7:9-17:

After this I looked, and there was a great multitude
that no one could count, from every nation, from all
tribes and peoples and languages, standing before
the throne and before the Lamb, robed in white,
with palm branches in their hands. [10]They cried
out in a loud voice, saying, "Salvation belongs to our
God who is seated on the throne, and to the Lamb!"
[11]And all the angels stood around the throne and
around the elders and the four living creatures, and
they fell on their faces before the throne and worshiped God, [12]singing, "Amen! Blessing and glory
and wisdom and thanksgiving and honor and power
and might be to our God forever and ever! Amen."
[13]Then one of the elders addressed me, saying,
"Who are these, robed in white, and where have
they come from?" [14]I said to him, "Sir, you are the
one that knows." Then he said to me, "These are

they who have come out of the great ordeal; they
have washed their robes and made them white in
the blood of the Lamb. [15]For this reason they are
before the throne of God, and worship him day and
night within his temple, and the one who is seated
on the throne will shelter them. [16]They will hunger
no more, and thirst no more; the sun will not strike
them, nor any scorching heat; [17]for the Lamb at
the center of the throne will be their shepherd, and
he will guide them to springs of the water of life,
and God will wipe away every tear from their eyes."

Because these two passages are future-oriented—because they take place in heaven—we tend to think that they
have little to do with what we are experiencing here today,
or with how we are to understand our present situation.
They are pretty words of comfort and inspiration, and that
is about all they can offer us. But the truth is that this vision
of the future is crucial if we are to understand how John of
Patmos sees his own situation vis-à-vis the many tribes and
peoples and nations and languages that worship the beast,
and on whom the great harlot is seated. And it is also true
that, if we are to understand today's multicultural pressures
and opportunities as John of Patmos would have us understand them, we too need a vision of the future similar to his.

My father-in-law was an avid reader of mystery stories.
He had walls and walls of bookcases with nothing but mys-
teries. He was the family expert on mystery novels, but we
used to make fun of the way he read them. Whenever he
got a new book, he would immediately turn to the last chapter and read it. Then he would go back to the beginning and
see how the author got to the intended end.

It is a strange way to read a mystery. Although that way of reading mystery stories has much to commend it, our modern mind rebels against it. We tend to look at things from beginning to end: from past, to present, to future. If you want to understand something, you study the previous events that produced it. We even have a phrase that we use when we think we understand someone: "I know where you are coming *from*."

What has made this view particularly prevalent in modern society is the success of the physical sciences. In the physical sciences, to "understand" something is to be able to explain its causes. And, when we today speak of "cause," we mean what the ancients called "efficient cause." The efficient cause of a billiard ball's moving into a pocket is that another ball hit it. And the efficient cause of that other ball's movement was that the cue hit it. And the efficient cause of the cue . . . and so on, and on, always backwards, into the past, to find the cause of things.

But that is not the only way to look at reality. In fact, throughout much of history most of humankind has believed that things are ultimately caused not so much by other events as by a purpose; not so much by their beginning as by their end. This is what medieval philosophers called the "final cause," or the "teleological cause." Things happen, not merely because something happened before, but also and above all because they are being called from a future toward which they are moving. Thus, when medieval philosophers said that God was the ultimate "cause" of the universe, they meant not only that in the beginning God made all things and set them in motion, as a first efficient cause, but also that God calls all things from the future, as their ultimate teleological cause.

We may find this difficult to understand, because to us "cause and effect" is a sequence that follows along chronological lines, always from the past, to the present, to the future. As mentioned above, this view has been profoundly influenced by the practical success of the physical sciences, which are precisely sciences that study efficient causes.

The truth is, however, that we do not really live our lives only on the basis of efficient causes. The reason why I am now sitting at my computer is not only that I came into my office and turned the switch on. The reason, at a much deeper level, is that I envision a book that will result from my sitting at the computer. The teleological cause is closer to the truth: I am sitting here, not just because the past has pushed me here, but also and above all because there is a future that has pulled me here.

And so it is with all of us. When we leave our driveway, we determine which way to turn on the basis of where we are going—in other words, the future is the cause of our decision. In truth, when we say "I know where you are coming from," what we really mean is "I know what you are getting at."

A good analogy for all of this is my father-in-law's way of reading a mystery book by beginning at the end. From the point of view of purely efficient causes, that is a crazy way to read a book. But it is probably much closer to the way the book was written. Most likely, the author decided on the solution long before the first word of the book was ever written. The entire book, from cover to cover, makes clearer sense when you read the story, not simply as the result of dozens of separate events that unfold in chronological order, but rather as the result of that final event, which pulls all the rest to itself. If we read the book from page 1 to the last page, it is not until the last page that we find that the butler did it. But if we get a glimpse of that last page, as my father-in-law was wont to do, then while reading the book we understand things differently. When the phone rings on page 5, or when the turkey burns on page 50, we have a sense of the meaning and purpose of those events in the mind of the author, in light of the fact that the butler did it.

In a way, this is also true of creation and history. We can study creation in all its details, limiting ourselves to efficient causes, and think we understand it. We can study historical events thoroughly according to their efficient causes, and think we understand them. But that is like reading the book from page 1, and coming to page 50 where the turkey burns. We understand that the turkey burns because it was too long in the oven. But in truth, the reason why the turkey burns on page 50 is because on page 250 we are to be told that the butler did it. Likewise, we understand neither creation nor history until we have a glimpse of the end for which creation was made, and the purpose toward which history is moving.

Not only do we make present decisions on the basis of the future we envision; we also read the past in the light of that future. This should be obvious to anyone who examines a few history textbooks. The history of Europe is not the same when read in Nazi Germany, in post-colonial Nigeria, in industrialized Japan, or in present-day Iraq. When we in the United States read the story of the Pilgrims and the Mayflower, part of what we find is raw data on which most would agree; but we also find much that reflects the future for which we hope as a nation.

In 1991, my wife and I visited first Spain, and then Mexico. In Spain, near the place from which Columbus sailed, there was a sign: "October 12, 1492. Five hundred years of the evangelization of the Americas." On the wall of the cathedral in Mexico City there was another sign: "October 12, 1492, day of national disaster." Both signs were about Columbus, but the one in Spain was reclaiming a sense of "manifest destiny" and a future of a special, perhaps somewhat patronizing, relationship with Spain's former colonies, while the one in Mexico was envisioning a future nation built around the revival and reaffirmation of ancestral cultures. In summary, the future guides both our present activity and our reading of the past.

This is one reason why the book of Revelation is so enthralling. We think that the book is mysterious because it speaks a language and uses symbols that are difficult to understand. We think that the book is mysterious because it speaks of bowls of wrath, and angels with trumpets, and seven seals, and four strange living creatures. But the book is mysterious in a deeper sense than that. The book is mysterious, paradoxically enough, because it declares what the early church announced openly: that when the final trumpet sounds, loud voices in heaven will proclaim: "The kingdom of the world has become the kingdom of our Lord and of his Messiah, and he will reign forever and ever" (11:15). And not only the Lamb, but also its servants, who are now brought low and persecuted, they too "will reign forever and ever" (22:5). When we read from this end, we can look at the present time, when the beast holds sway and is worshiped by the peoples, tribes, and nations, in a different way.

John's message is not ultimately about a beast whose number is 666, nor about seven bowls of wrath. John's message is about the goal and end of history, about the purpose of the world, about the final cause of all that exists, about the fact that, even in spite of beasts coming out of the land and of the sea, and in spite of the great harlot sitting on many waters, and in spite of people from all nations and tribes and languages being willing to serve the beast, in spite of all this, God and God's Messiah, the Lamb who was slain, will reign forever and ever.

And John's message is also that, in that everlasting reign of God, "saints from every tribe and language and people and nation" will be made "a kingdom and priests serving our God" (5:9-10); that these will be "a great multitude that no one could count, from every nation, from all tribes and peoples and languages, standing before the throne and before the Lamb, robed in white, with palm branches in their hands ... [crying] out in a loud voice saying, 'Salvation belongs to our God who is seated on the throne, and to the Lamb!'" (7:9-10). In the book of Daniel, the same peoples and nations of every language who at first adored the image in the end are commanded by Darius to "tremble and fear before the God of Daniel." In Revelation, people from the same tribes, nations, and languages that formerly worshiped the beast in the end are part of the throng worshiping the Lamb who was slain and the One sitting on the throne.

The phrase, *from* every tribe and nation, thus has two meanings. In the first place, it has the meaning which we most commonly ascribe to it: in the end, when God's will is accomplished, those who praise God and the Lamb will be "from every tribe and nation and people and language." But then there is another meaning which follows from this: *from* every tribe and nation means that this is the vision from which, out of which, the church must live. The church lives not only out of its past, but also out of its future; not only out of its efficient cause, but also out of its final cause. It draws not only from its beginning, but also from its end. And, if its beginning was multicultural, as the story of Pentecost clearly shows, its end is also multicultural, as John's vision also shows with equal clarity.

Reading these two passages of John's vision of God's future, I feel as my father-in-law must have felt when he opened the last chapter of a mystery novel. Aha! The butler did it! So that is what it is all about! Aha! A kingdom of God, where God and the Lamb shall reign forever. A kingdom drawn from all tribes and peoples and nations and languages, where they shall all be a royal priesthood. A kingdom where they shall wear their white robes of victory and wave palms of jubilation, celebrating the victory of the Lamb in a multitude of languages, for they are people from every tribe and nation. That is what it is all about!

According to the book of Revelation, that is what it is all about. And if that is what it is all about, that had better be what the church is about. If we really believe that this is the future toward which God's history is moving, we had better live out of that future, and not out of some other.

When the church refuses to live out of that future, its witness is hardly credible. In many ways, such witness is like a dialogue I might have with a friend:

My friend says: "I can hardly wait till I retire. As soon as I retire, I plan to spend all my time fishing. I am going to move to the woods, build myself a little cabin where no one will bother me, and where there will be no sound but the rustling of a brook. I am going to spend hours sitting quietly leaning against a tree, feeling the breeze on my face and smelling the flowers. I can hardly wait till I can retire and spend the rest of my days fishing."

"What do you do now in your free time?" I would ask. Imagine then a reply such as: "Oh, I spend my time in the stock car races. Actually, I am even building my own hot rod!" I would either laugh or bemoan my friend's self-delusion, because there is an incongruity between his professed future and the way he is preparing for it. Most likely, in spite of all his enthusiastic talk about fishing by a quiet brook, deep down he does not really believe that he will ever live in a cabin in the woods.

But then, think about Christians. Think about the church. We spend so much time talking about the coming Reign of God. We pray repeatedly, "Thy Kingdom come." To hear some of our sermons, and to read some of our books, one would imagine that we can hardly wait for the Reign of God to come. But, are we preparing for the time when God's Reign does come? We proclaim a Reign in which the last shall be first. Yet, when I look at the church I see many of us competing to be ahead of everybody else with just as much zeal as that in an Olympic competition. We proclaim a Reign of peace, a Reign of justice, a Reign of love. But, are we living as those whose future is there?

If my friend claims that he plans to spend the rest of his life fishing by a quiet brook, and meanwhile spends his time building hot rods, the first and most immediate result will be that no one will believe him. If he really wants to convince me that fishing by a rustling brook is so great, he had better begin by going fishing as often as he can, so that I may be convinced of his purposes by his actions. If we really want the world to believe the proclamation of the Reign of God, then, both as individuals and as a church, we had better begin living as a people that is practicing for that Reign.

Then, there is a second result. If the time comes when my friend does move to a cabin in the woods, and he has not been practicing for it, the woods will not be all that great. He will not know how to manage in the woods. Every unexpected sound will startle and scare him. He will not know how to cook the fish that he catches, and he will get indigestion from the fish he tries to cook. He will get cramps from sitting on the ground, leaning against a tree. Likewise, one could surmise that if we do not practice for the Reign of God now, we shall be rather uncomfortable when the Reign does come!

Clearly, the vision of the Reign of God has important socio-political implications. It was so at the time of John of Patmos, and it is so today. In John's time, Rome saw itself as the great city, the great builder of cities, the great "cityfier" —or, as we would say today, civilizer. The Roman vision was that of a world dotted with cities, all patterned after Rome and all submissive to Rome. Where ancient cities already existed, they were rebuilt, embellished, often granted special privileges. Where there were no cities, the Romans built new ones. This was their great pride, so that when Aelius Aristides, the famous orator from Smyrna, visited Rome and sought to praise her for her achievements, he did so by boasting that "the coasts and interiors have been filled with cities."

John's vision is also that of a great city—a city so great that next to it Rome is not even a hamlet. John speaks of a city of justice and peace, where God will wipe away every tear from people's eyes, and death will be no more; a city whose gates never close, because it is open to all the tribes, and languages, and peoples; a city in whose midst is the tree of life whose leaves are for the healing of the nations; a city that welcomes and accepts the contributions of all the kings of the earth. If that is the city which God promises and John sees, that promise and that vision are a challenge to the great city of Rome, sitting over many waters, a city within whose walls and throughout whose empire there is violence and poverty. If the city of Rome claimed to be the great civilizer, the great cityfier, John and those around him looked forward to a new city, not built by Rome—a city where, in contrast to the squalid conditions of the urban masses, and to the violence which ruled in earthly cities then and now, "death will be no more; mourning and crying and pain will be no more."

Just as John's vision was a challenge to Rome's vision, so it is also a challenge to our cities, cities of alabaster buildings gleaming over the homeless huddled under bridges, cities where death walks the streets at night, where children live in fear and the most common visions are the hallucinations of addicts and alcoholics. Furthermore, if John's vision is true, and a great city of love and peace is a proper image for describing God's future for humankind, what does that say about those of us who have decided that the only way to enjoy life in peace is to abandon the city to its own misery, to create our own suburban sectarian little "new Jerusalems" where we can live in peace while our cities burn?

Contrary to what we might expect, and in contrast with much of its later history, the church in the changing society of the first century, rather than simply bemoaning change, posited and announced even greater change. Let others complain that Rome has become a cesspool for the scum of the world. Let others seek refuge in their exurban villas. John calls Christians in Ephesus, Smyrna, and the other cities of Asia to continue living in those cities as those whose citizenship is in the New Jerusalem.

Clearly, John's vision is radical, and it provides ample fodder for the social activist. But, significantly, John's vision combines what we today would call social well-being with something for which many social activists have little use, the worship of God:

> After this I looked, and there was a great multitude that no one could count, from every nation, from all tribes and peoples and languages, standing before the throne and before the Lamb, robed in white, with palm branches in their hands.... They are before the throne of God, and worship him day and night within his temple, and the one who is seated on the throne will shelter them. They will hunger no more, and thirst no more; the sun will not strike them, nor any scorching heat; for the Lamb at the center of the throne will be their shepherd, and he will guide them to springs of the water of life, and God will wipe away every tear from their eyes. (Rev 7:9, 15-17)

This may seem strange to many of us, modern pragmatists who have been taught that the purpose of worship is to recharge our batteries on Sunday so that we can go out and reform the world on Monday. But John of Patmos would agree with the followers of John Calvin and the entire Reformed tradition that the chief end of human beings, and indeed of all creation, is to enjoy God and to glorify God forever.[1]

---

[1]*Shorter Catechism*, q. 1: "What is the chief end of man? Man's chief end is to glorify God, and to enjoy him forever." Thomas Aquinas would agree: "All things are ordered, as if to an end, to the supreme good, which is God." *Summa contra gentiles*, 3.17.

Worship is much more than an act whereby we re-charge our spiritual batteries. If it is true that our chief end is to glorify God forever, then worship is first of all an act of justice. It is an act of justice because it puts things in their right place, and only inasmuch as it puts things in their right place. Justice among humans, without rendering to God what is God's due, is always partial justice, and therefore in-justice. And, as the prophets of Israel repeatedly said, to pretend to worship God without doing justice in society is to worship a god who does not require justice, which is to worship a false god—to practice idolatry. In the biblical view, worship requires justice, and worship also is justice. Worship requires justice, for the God of the Bible is a God who does not care about our religious fasts and feasts if they are not accompanied by justice. And worship is justice, be-cause it puts creature and Creator in their just relationship, without which all other relationships falter. As the Roman Missal and the old Book of Common Prayer instructed, when we are called to give thanks to God the very first thing we must remember and acknowledge is that "it is meet and right so to do."

Worship is also an act of rehearsal. It is an anticipation of things to come. It is the moment at which we are remind-ed that our lives and our world have a goal, and that this goal is that day when every nation and tribe and people and language will worship God and the Lamb. It must be a fore-taste, within our small community of worship, of that great city, the New Jerusalem, which John saw coming down from heaven, from God. It is practice for the Kingdom. It is a foretaste of the Reign of God.

Worship is also an act of proclamation. In worship, we show the unbelieving world its own goal and future. Paul refs to this in 1 Corinthians when he says that every time we celebrate communion we proclaim the Lord's death until He comes. Likewise, every time we gather for worship we proclaim the great, final gathering at the river, the coming of the New Jerusalem, the day when "a great multitude that no one can count, from every nation, from all tribes and peoples and languages, standing before the throne and before the Lamb, robed in white, with palm branches in their hands," will worship God day and night, and "God will shelter them, and they will hunger no more, and thirst no more."

Worship is a rehearsal and an act of proclamation. For both reasons, in order to rehearse and in order to proclaim, the church must make every effort to make certain that here and now, as there and then, "every nation and tribe and people and language" be present and represented; that no one be excluded or diminished because of their tribe, or nation, or people, or language.

That is why, faced by an empire that he could describe only in terms of an apocalyptic beast, John gave us a book whose culminating vision is the liturgy that takes place in heaven. In that respect, the book of Revelation is very strange indeed. In no book of the New Testament are there more references to singing and to worship. Yet the book of Revelation does not give even one directive for worship. Paul tells the Corinthians that when they celebrate their meal they should wait for each other, and gives them some directives for doing things decently and in order. He tells the Colossians to "sing psalms, hymns, and spiritual songs to God" (Col 3:16). In Leviticus and in other portions of the Hebrew Scriptures there are many directives for worship. But in Revelation—the book where the four living creatures that represent all of creation sing day and night without ceasing, the book where the twenty-four elders fall before the one who is seated on the throne, casting down their crowns and worshiping the one who lives for ever and ever—there is not one word about how we should worship. There is no need for such a word, for the entire book is an announcement of the worship which takes place in heaven, the worship which is the ultimate end of all things, the worship toward which we are bound.

In that worship, saints from every tribe and people and nation and language take part.

There are alternative visions. There is a vision according to which all peoples and nations and tribes and languages must bow before the beast and worship it. This is the vision of Nebuchadnezzar: "You are commanded, O peoples, nations, and languages, that...you are to fall down and worship the golden statue that King Nebuchadnezzar has set up" (Dn 3:4-5). There is a vision that takes for granted that there will always be a great harlot who sits upon many waters; and these waters are the many nations and tribes and languages and peoples who must bring their wealth to her. In a way, this is the vision of Belshazzar in the book of Daniel, who does not learn from his father's humiliation, but is content with inheriting his power over peoples and nations. If we live by that vision, we shall be content with a world order in which many nations and tribes and peoples and cultures have no other purpose in life but to enrich those who sit upon many waters. According to that vision, the nations and peoples and tribes can and should remain subjected, for that is their place in the scheme of things. According to that vision, our task is to make sure that we, and others like us, are the ones who sit upon many waters, while the rest of the world enriches us.

But that is not the vision of John of Patmos. According to his vision, out of these many nations and tribes and peoples and languages, God will build a kingdom in which all have royal and priestly honor. According to that vision, a great multitude, from all different nations and cultures, will jointly sing, "Holy, Holy, Holy, Lord God Almighty." According to that vision, our music and our worship must be multicultural, not simply because our society is multicultural, but because the future from which God is calling us is multicultural. We must be multicultural, not just so that those from other cultures may feel at home among us, but also so that we may feel at home in God's future. We must be multicultural because, like John of Patmos, our eyes have seen the glory of the coming of the Lord; because we know and we believe that on that great waking-up morning when the stars begin to fall, when we gather at the river where angel feet have trod, we shall all, from all nations and tribes and peoples and languages, we shall all sing without ceasing: "Holy, holy, holy! All the saints adore thee, casting down our golden crowns before the glassy sea; cherubim and seraphim; Japanese and Swahili; American and European; Cherokee and Ukrainian; falling down before thee, who wert, and art, and evermore shall be!" Amen!

Index